They came as strangers
left as friends
etched forever in my heart.

Dedication

This book is dedicated to broadcaster Doug Williams who loved me like a daughter and taught me everything I know about radio and television. I don't believe it was coincidental I know it was in God's plan from the onset. Doug was meant to be my guardian angel here on earth. Every step of the way, he was there for me. He was my mentor and my best friend.

Working alongside Doug on "The Holiday Show" at WOLS Radio in Florence, South Carolina, was truly a gift. He also took me to WBTW-TV 13 and taught me the tricks of the trade. I looked forward to being with him and learning from him every single day during my first eight years out of college. Most of all, he taught me to respect every on-air guest.

Thanks to Doug, I have experienced a fulfilling career that is still going strong today. As a result, I have met so many wonderful people along the way who have brightened my life.

Doug Williams died in 2012, leaving a hole in my heart that can never be filled.

Doug Williams

Doug Williams was born Nathan Wesley Williams in the Willow Creek community of Florence, South Carolina.

From the time he was very young, he wanted to be a radio announcer. He even built himself a small studio in his yard where he pretended to read the news, relay the weather, and report the latest community events. Neighbors thought it was an outhouse, but it was the beginning of something big for Doug.

After high school in 1950 Doug went to work for WOLS in Florence followed by a short stint at WACA in Camden, South Carolina.

He was drafted a year later into the Marine Corps and served at Cherry Point, North Carolina where he became a war correspondent handling radio communications and DJ responsibilities for the only Marine Corps Radio station in the world, WCPR. He continued to work for WOLS Radio returning to Florence for weekend shifts.

Doug then took a job at WBLR in Batesville-Leesville and a short romp at WDKD in Kingstree. He had gotten the nickname "The Bashful Bachelor" but this came to a quick halt when he married the love of his life, Sylvia Hatchell.

Doug was then hired a third and final time by WOLS, a tenure that lasted fifty years. At this time the station was owned by FBI G-Man, Melvin Purvis who lived in Florence. Throughout his career, Doug loved telling folks about the sweet and easy demeanor of Purvis compared to his vigilance in capturing John Dillinger.

While at WOLS, Doug sold advertising as well as spinning records but his claim to fame was certainly when he created "The Holiday Show" in 1960, a public affairs broadcast that gave anyone a forum to talk about anything.

Politicians, celebrities, business owners, all loved the "come anytime" live, ninety-minute format that lasted twenty-eight years.

Doug warmly welcomed every guest and treated each one with total respect.

During this time, Doug also served as a newscaster and weather reporter for WBTW-TV 13, appearing in many commercials and hosting telethons.

He won many local broadcasting awards for his on-air work, his community support, and for his mentoring of many younger announcers.

The Sertoma Club presented Doug with their "Service To Mankind" award, and on December 21, 1999 Florence City Council declared it "Doug Williams Day".

Once WOLS Radio was sold, Doug hosted a TV show for eight and a half years at WELY in Florence. He enjoyed TV but always missed the magic of radio.

Upon retirement, Doug enjoyed spending more time with Sylvia, his daughter Debra, her husband Dennis and his two grandchildren.

Ironically, a few years after his retirement, Doug received the biggest honor of his career when the South Carolina Broadcaster's Association named him "The Master's Award" winner for 2005.

Doug Williams died at eighty-three years old on
June 22, 2012.

Florence was a more beautiful place thanks to Doug's golden voice, which was only surpassed by his golden heart.

Acknowledgements

Chuck, my wonderful and patient husband, best friend, and business partner for the past thirty-one years, you are simply amazing. Thank you for not laughing when I told you I was going to write a book! I could never have done it without your computer expertise and helpful suggestions. I thank God every day for the blessing you are in my life.

Mom, you have always been my head cheerleader and biggest fan. It is because of you that I have grown to become the confident and somewhat offbeat woman I am today. It is you who taught me to "live, love, and laugh."

I am so grateful to all my many friends and family who encouraged me to write this book and document the stories of my career. A special thank you goes to author and food writer Becky Billingsley for all the free advice she gave me on how to give birth to a book. Caroline Evans, although very busy with her own writing schedule, jumped in as proofreader and corrected my silly mistakes. After all, it's been a long time since I was in English class. I was very fortunate to choose Bob O'Brien of Prose Press from Pawleys Island as my publisher. Bob's expertise has helped many local authors like myself make their publishing dreams come true.

Muchos Gracias to J.P. Perez of Hair Safari who keeps me looking sassy!

Thanks to all those whose photography captured the crazier moments of my career. Please forgive me if I did not give you a photo credit, as it was hard to recall who gave me each picture after all these years!

Finally, to each and every one I interviewed over the past forty-two years, know that you began as my guest but left as my friend.

Table of Contents

Celebrity Stories

Local Treasures

My Career Journey

"Floating On Air" just seemed like the perfect name for my book. "On Air" of course reflects my radio and TV career. In broadcasting when you are in front of the microphone or camera it is said that you are on the air, and since I have enjoyed every minute of it, I have truly been floating for forty-two years. Coming up with a book title is never easy but when I checked the thesaurus for "Floating On Air" it referenced words and phrases like cheerful, contented, overjoyed, lighthearted, exhilarated, pleased as punch, and gratified. I had found the absolutely perfect title.

One of my favorite movies is "City Slickers." In it, Billy Crystal works for a radio station selling advertising. In one scene Billy realizes that his son is embarrassed by what he does for a living. Billy asks, "What's wrong with what I do?" His son replies, "I can't tell my friends that you sell air for a living!" Well, just as Billy's character was selling air, I have made a living "Floating On Air."

Local TV is not what people think it is. Everyone sees it as glamorous, big bucks, prestigious. It's none of those things. However, this is all I have done for my entire career. Most TV folks begin their careers by moving up the ladder constantly to bigger markets. Except for me. That was never my goal. Oh sure, I thought about it from time to time, even had a few fabulous offers, but I was so happy and contented being near family and friends.

My entry into broadcasting was unique. While I was in high school, I was invited to go on a local radio show, "The Holiday Show," with Doug Williams and talk about the local youth council. Doug took a liking to me, as they say in these parts, and invited me to come back and visit the show anytime. The next year, I was selected to represent the Florence Civitan Club at Wild Acres, a humanitarian camp in the mountains of North Carolina. The week following the camp, I was invited to speak to the Civitans about this experience and on that same night the Florence Civitans were presenting Doug Williams with the "Broadcaster of the Year" award. It was fortuitous. Doug commented on how well I spoke to the crowd and told me he wanted me to co-host his show when I finished all my schooling.

That was 1968. I was a junior in high school and all I wanted to do was write, not talk. From the time I was a kid, I had won poetry awards, writing awards, received straight As in literary arts, but never once did I consider a career in broadcasting. At that time, there were few female role models. I remember Jessica Savitch, the NBC television reporter who was killed in a car accident early in her career, and even Barbara Walters who made her way into the scene in the early '60s, but that was pretty much it! Female television personalities were few and far between. My goal was to study journalism and become a writer for newspapers and magazines. I loved asking questions and talking to strangers. As a matter of fact, my grandmother used to say I was too darn friendly for my own good! When she took me shopping on the bus in Newark, New Jersey, as a kid, I talked to all the folks on the bus and before we got off at our destination I knew their life histories.

In 1969, I graduated from McClenaghan High School in Florence, being voted "The Most Friendly" out of 488 students. Then I attended the Florence campus of the University of South Carolina, majoring in journalism and minoring in sociology. But at the end of my sophomore year, the school became Francis Marion College and they dropped the journalism major. I considered transferring to USC in Columbia, where I had won a scholarship, but by this time I was engrained on the campus as head cheerleader, vice president of my class, president of the Collegiate Civitan Club, and more. I just could not leave the Francis Marion campus I had grown to love, nor move away from my parents and sister.

Within months, President Walter D. Smith chose me to become the student representative to the media. When media reps wanted to talk about the campus and ask what it was like attending a new four-year institution, I did the interview and simultaneously obtained a world of experience.

Upon graduation, I went to work writing for a local tourism magazine that was new and fledgling. After six months, the job fizzled out and I had to go to the South Carolina Labor Board to fight for back wages – not what I expected from my first job out of school. It was then that Doug Williams called me to co-host "the Holiday Show" on WOLS Radio. It was part-time, just an hour and half each morning Monday through Friday broadcasting live from the Holiday Inn Downtown (which is now the sight of the beautiful Florence Performing Arts Center). During my time at WOLS, ("SLOW" spelled backward), the station was owned by Melvin Purvis' sons. In the 1930s, Melvin was the lead FBI agent for the Chicago office and was involved in the capturing of more public enemies than any other agent in FBI history, including Baby Face Nelson, Pretty Boy Floyd, and John Dillinger. The WOLS team was one big happy family, all wonderful people who loved Florence and wanted the best for the community.

It was during this time Doug took me out to WBTW-TV 13, which was the only TV station in the market, and carried ABC and CBS programming. Doug taught me how to record voice-overs for commercials, which in turn led to lots of on-camera work. Doug did this so unselfishly. He could have recorded these spots himself and received the talent fee, but he wanted to expand my broadcasting talents. He taught me how to work the equipment that was mind-boggling to me at the time. He taught me how to erase mistakes and how to label the cartridges. Doug Williams was my mentor as well as my best friend. He led me into the broadcasting world and gave me the confidence to continue. Best of all, we were magical together. He was the straight guy and I was the silly one. Even though he was old enough to be my dad, we had a chemistry that is not easily found in co-hosts and we met so many incredible folks during our partnership. (Please see the chapter on commercials.)

Two months after starting the radio job, Doug encouraged me to talk to Mr. Joe Foster, the general manager of WBTW. Doug said I'd be the perfect person to start a show for women, as they already had a talk show hosted by Johnny Andrucci, who was occasionally joined by local dress shop owner, Mary Cutter. I'll never forget what Mr. Foster said when I went to talk to him: "We don't want women in TV!" He'd have been sued if he said that today; however, he was known for his abruptness.

There was only one other time that I almost lost a job because I was a woman and that was in 1971 when I worked in the ladies wear department for Treasure City Department store in Florence. It was Thanksgiving Day and Santa Claus was supposed to arrive by helicopter and parachute onto the roof of the store while thousands of kids waited in the parking lot to see him. This particular year, Santa did not show up for work because he had a hangover from the night before. The manager, Mr. Atlas, was frantic as he did not know anyone who could fill in at the last minute, and it was mostly women who worked at the store. That's where I offered to save the day. Mr. Atlas insisted I was being ridiculous and said only a man could be Santa.

However, fifteen minutes later, which was only thirty minutes from Santa's scheduled appearance, Mr. Atlas decked me out in cotton batting from the notions department and I became the "First Woman Santa Claus." After the *Florence Morning News* did a story on it, followed by a story in newspapers across the country thanks to The Associated Press, the entire country knew about it. The story ran as a woman's lib feature, even though it had nothing to do with it. The article featured me in a bathing suit from the "Miss Florence" Pageant that ran in the *Florence Morning News* earlier that year. Next to the bathing suit photo was me in the Santa suit. I received proposals from men in jail, letters from women cheering me on, and yes, even an offer from *Playboy* magazine.

It was my fifteen minutes of fame. However, I was so good

at the job that I not only finished the entire Christmas as Santa, using my deep cheerleader voice to disguise I was a woman, I was asked back the following year to do it all over again. Both years it was simply joyful to hold those little ones on my lap and take their requests.

Once I knew I was not going to get a job with WBTW other than commercials and hosting telethons, I happened to mention my need for some full-time work to John Smith, the general manager of the Holiday Inn where Doug and I did "The Holiday Show." Bingo! I became the director of sales and public relations for two Holiday Inns in Florence, owned by Servico Corporation. The salary was better than I expected and offered great benefits and lots of experience. I was sent to other cities to work with their sales people and even had a chance to speak to the students at the University of Florida about the importance of public relations. These two jobs took me from 1973-1981. However, broadcasting had become my passion.

One of the most painful things I ever had to do was to tell Doug that the new ABC affiliate, WPDE-TV 15, had offered me a full-time job hosting, producing, and selling advertising for their new talk show, "Pee Dee People." Yet once again, Doug was happy for me. He always said he hated that my salary was "peanuts," but we both knew it was the Holiday Inn job that enabled me to continue with the part-time radio and freelance TV gigs. The truth of the matter is when I left the Holiday Inn, I took a $14,000 cut in pay, a loss of extraordinary benefits and stock options, to follow my heart and accept the job at WPDE.

From 1981-1984 I was the talk show host, producer, and salesperson for "Pee Dee People," a public affairs broadcast featuring local events, authors, chefs, and topics of interest throughout the area. To keep the show on the air, I had to go out and get advertisers, and I did.

Once a week on "Pee Dee People," I opened the phone lines for free advice from various professionals from our viewing area and it led to some of my most embarrassing TV moments.

During this time, I even got to host and produce a live on-air auction featuring our many advertisers that proved very successful for the station, and the best thing that happened to me while at WPDE is that I met my husband Chuck. He was a commercial producer who came to work in 1983. We made many commercials together and fell in love. We like to say we were the first real "love affair" but not the first affair at Channel 15.

However, the entire time I was at the station, General Manager Jerry Condra begged me to consider anchoring the news. He knew I had local appeal having been in Florence since I was fourteen years old, and I was very involved in the community. He even offered me a salary that would have doubled my income, because after all the news makes profits, talk shows don't. But having co-hosted "The Holiday Show" for seven and a half years, I knew my talents, my desires, and what I did best. I had a passion for interviewing, not reading cue cards and teleprompters.

My favorite interviews were not newsy at all, but either funny or poignant. I knew news was not my forte. Mr. Condra's persistence became annoying. I was a good friend with the female co-anchor and it would have hurt her tremendously to be taken from the anchor position even though she was also the news director and probably would have remained in that position.

Meanwhile, a former employee of WPDE who was now in Sacramento, California, offered me a job as a PM Magazine host. The salary was three times what I was currently earning. The clothing allowance alone was more than I was making at WPDE. But I was a homebody. My parents, younger sister, and the community meant the world to me and I could not take the job. California was beautiful, but it was not where I wanted to be. It was an honor to be offered such a prestigious position with big bucks, but I never looked back.

Finally in 1984, my show was going to be off the air due to the summer Olympics on ABC. I signed off, saying I would be back in two weeks. However, that afternoon Mr. Condra called me into his office and gave me an ultimatum: take the news anchor position or I would have no job at all because he was canceling my show. He actually thought he could con me into doing something I did not want to do. He even reminded me that I was getting married in a few weeks and needed the job. Plus, he said that I would not be able to get another television job in the market because of a non-compete clause in my contract. I reminded him that if he were canceling my show, a non-compete agreement would not hold up in court. Then, I simply stood up and said, "Mr. Condra, thanks for the offer, but since my contract says I was hired to host and produce a talk show, I guess I'm done here." Then he started to back pedal, begging me to stay but refusing the talk show position, only offering the news. I left his office, went to mine and started packing my stuff, trying not to cry. Then I stuck my head into my future husband's office to quickly tell him what just happened. He was not shocked because he knew I was being pressured for years to take on the news desk.

The next few days were tough. I cried a lot. I loved that show and had given it blood, sweat, and tears. Stockholders from the station who all watched me grow up in Florence called and asked what really happened. I told them the truth, and I know Mr. Condra's relationship with the staff, investors, and community suffered from it all. It was big news since WPDE and WBTW were in a ratings war. The *Florence Morning News* headlines the next day said it all – "The Ratings War Begins; Pee Dee People, the First Fatality." Tons of letters to the editor came pouring in supporting me and praising the show, but Mr. Condra was not backing down.

He even sent me a letter reminding me that I could not work in local media due to my contract. A lawyer friend, Delton Powers of Bennettsville, who had appeared on "Southern Style" many times offering free legal advice to the viewers, came to my rescue. He sent Mr. Condra a letter confirming my belief: a canceled contract by the station meant I was free to pursue whatever means I could to get a job. Any further threats would result in a lawsuit. Case closed. Thank you, Delton!

Within the next two weeks, I was offered all types of jobs: on-camera video work for commercials; handling publicity for various businesses; two Wilmington stations offered me work, but sadly more news jobs, no talk show. My best job offer came from a State Farm Agency in New Bern, North Carolina, a position that would have made me a six-figure woman in no time flat and the first female agent in North Carolina. Heck, I'm still not a six-figure woman, but insurance was not what I wanted to do. It was not my field nor expertise and for me, it has never been about money.

Chuck and I had talked about wanting to live in Myrtle Beach someday. We both loved the ocean. We knew there was some talk about stations opening offices there, but figured we would never leave our current positions at the time. Now, since I did not have a job, and was making twice the salary Chuck was making, which wasn't saying much, we really did not have a lot to lose. So we prayed about it and there was no doubt that God and our hearts were leading us to Myrtle Beach.

Enter Doug Williams AGAIN, my dear friend. He owned a small, 800-square-foot house that he built in Cherry Grove. It had no heat because it was used as a summer place, but Doug offered it to us rent-free for as long as we needed it. Then a friend who formerly worked at WPDE with us offered us a chance to help her market the new mausoleums at Hillcrest Cemetery with the well-known and beloved Goldfinch family. We definitely did not want to do this forever, but if it could help us make ends meet until jobs in our field opened up, we figured we would try it. Plus WWAY in Wilmington was promising me a talk show and a feature reporter position out of Myrtle Beach, so there were irons in the fire.

The week after our honeymoon in October 1984, we moved to Cherry Grove with our four cats while we stored most of our furniture. We were off and running except we hated the job at Hillcrest. Dreaded it. These were wonderful folks to work with but it was too depressing for both of us.

Three months later, Kathy D'Antoni of WCOX, a small operation that provided local programming for Cox Cable customers in Myrtle Beach, offered me my own show, which would start March 5, 1985. I was ecstatic. I did not care how small this audience was, it was a job and I was going to get to do something I loved, again! We clinched the deal that day. "Southern Style" was born and lived on for twenty-three years. We were live at 10 a.m. Monday through Friday and repeated nightly at 7:30 p.m., fielding phone calls and similar topics as I had previously done on "Pee Dee People." I absolutely loved it. A few years into the stint, the producer quit and I got a slight raise to produce the show as well, which simply meant booking the guests.

Then one night in June, Nat Adams, the production manager on WCOX, begged me to come to Studebakers dance club to host the dance show Cox Cable had been producing. The current host was demanding a raise, and said he was not showing up unless he got one! I tried to get out of it as I was highly allergic to smoke and of course the clubs were filled with it back then. But Nat was desperate and the show must go on, right? I had no idea what I was getting into as I had never even seen the show, but I wound up loving it!

"Studebakers Live" was a weekly, high-adrenaline dance competition featuring everything from rock 'n' roll to two-stepping country dancers. We taped it on Thursday nights all summer long and it aired on both Saturday and Sunday nights at 7. So it was not actually live but it was taped live, as there was very little editing. I took allergy meds to help me get through each taping but how could I give up a show that literally everyone watched and anxiously awaited week after week. What a high!

During my tenure of hosting it, Cox Cable got a letter from Arbitron, the folks who do television ratings, and they said that Horry County was the only place in the nation where there were more people watching "Studebakers Live" on Sunday nights than watching CBS's "60 Minutes." "Studebakers Live" amazingly beat the nationally acclaimed "60 Minutes" in the ratings for Horry

County.

For seven years I hosted and produced the Studebaker dance contest, even recruiting prizes for the contestants and working with all the sponsors, until Don Cauthen, the club owner, decided he was not making the kind of money he wanted with the show and pulled the plug. (Please see my story on a risqué episode of "Studebakers Live.")

However, while I was doing these two shows for Cox Cable, Chuck was hired by Bruce Miller of WBTW-TV 13 in Florence as the first production manager for their new Myrtle Beach office. Yahoo! We were on a roll.

WBTW's first office was at the old Holiday Inn West in two small hotel rooms. Every afternoon the "live truck" would come up from Florence to Myrtle Beach, pull into the parking lot at the Holiday Inn West, hook up the camera and microphone, and they were on the air with Sherena Gainey reporting live from the beach. Compared to their state-of-the-art Myrtle Beach studio today, it was humble beginnings. But once they had established the Myrtle Beach office, Bruce offered me a show, "The Coastal Real Estate Video Guide" that featured local condo projects, housing developments, and realtors. Those being interviewed paid to be on, but sadly the show only lasted for a year. In 1985 this show was simply before its time, but since Chuck directed it, we had a blast putting it all together each week.

Next, WBTW offered me a Sunday morning magazine format show called "Grand Strand Gazette." It aired right after Charles Kuralt's Sunday morning program, so it had a great audience. Chuck became the director; Terri Brobst our camera operator, editor, and partner in crime; I served as host and producer. We were a dynamic threesome getting the show shot and edited week after week on top of all our other duties. (Please read my story about working on a promo with Charles Kuralt.)

I was very blessed to be hosting and producing three shows I dearly loved, all different but all right up my alley. Neither Cox Cable nor WBTW were bothered that I worked for them both, as they were not as competitive back then. However, "Grand

Strand Gazette" was canceled after three years because the sales team could not make it work financially. Very few advertisers wanted to run ads on Sunday morning.

Meanwhile, I took on a new challenge. Barbara Foster of Florence, the regional director for the March of Dimes, asked me to become the executive director for the March of Dimes of Horry and Georgetown counties. I had been a volunteer for this organization in high school and college so it seemed like a perfect fit. Traveling around the area to line up WalkAmerica, bachelor auctions, golf tournaments, and other fund-raisers, was fun and rewarding and I held the position for seven years until it became too much to handle in addition to my TV work.

Locally, Time Warner Cable purchased Cox Cable. Thankfully, "Southern Style" continued but the Time Warner production department got so busy with other obligations like producing commercials and other local shows that they insisted we do Monday's show live, then tape the other four immediately afterward. This made for a very stressful Monday. I was always very cautious that it did not appear to be a cattle call, running guests in and out all day long. I wanted each guest to feel special and not feel rushed. Let's face it, they were nervous enough. I literally sat with each one of them for ten minutes to review questions about their topics and explain the process before we started. I've always been a good talker, which helps when you host your own talk show, but I am equally a good "listener." Many talk-show hosts are too busy thinking of their next question and are not really paying attention to what their guest is saying, and run the risk of asking a question the guest has already answered or missed an opportunity to ask a relevant follow-up question. Listening is one of the most important talents in the talk-show business. Listen closely to your guest and don't worry what comes next.

"Southern Style" ran for twenty-three years until Mary Ann Moore, a former Time Warner manager in Myrtle Beach, who was now working at Time Warner's office in Columbia, canceled it. She created her own statewide TV show, but had no experience in doing so and insisted the Myrtle Beach production crew go on the road with her. It was painful. After all those years, I learned about the cancellation in a certified letter from her, rather than in person. Even a phone call would have been better. It was a total shock. I always heard from fellow employees that she was envious of me, but this was no way to handle the demise of the show. Fortunately, I was allowed to continue "Southern Style" until the end of the year and had a chance to say goodbye to my wonderful viewers. Mary Ann's show was short-lived and she no longer works for Time Warner Cable.

Going back to 1988 Chuck was still making very little money and was feeling frustrated at WBTW. With a master's degree in mass communication making less than $20,000 a year, he was fit to be tied. WPDE had also opened a Myrtle Beach office and everything was heating up. Competition between the two stations had everyone on edge.

I suggested we start our own business, perhaps a video production company where Chuck could continue shooting and editing commercials and venture into marketing videos. At the time there were only two other video production companies in town. Chuck asked me how we could start a business with no money in savings. "We can't do it on our looks," he said. And I said, "Yes we can." And yes we did! We went the next day to meet with a banker friend, Joe Alexander.

Stages Video Productions became the name of our new baby because our bank loan was in three stages and being the theatrical duo that we are, we tied the name into Shakespeare's line, "All the world's a stage." Chuck gave WBTW six months' notice, saying he was going to quit at the end of the year to start our own business, and they agreed to allow him to stay on until then.

This was the single best career move we both ever made. At TV stations, nothing is secure. Even with a contract, you can get the axe. And if the station gets sold, or a new station manager comes in, you can still feel threatened. Stages Video was the stability we needed to remain in Myrtle Beach for the rest of our lives without putting our careers in the hands of others. I became the majority owner and president even though Chuck was working the business full-time. I had several part-time jobs doing three different TV shows, but being a female-owned business qualified us for priority with state jobs and for borrowing money. Chuck was never bothered by that as he saw the positives in it all and knew that everyone in town knew me, so we could not go wrong.

We operated out of our home for more than a year, building capital and clients. Chapin Department Store became our first client. I had been their spokesperson for five years at that time and Chuck had made all their commercials while at WBTW. We loved all those folks and they loved us. This did not bother WBTW. For most TV stations, production charges are minimal or even free. Making the commercial is a loss leader. They make their money when the spot airs. The point was to get the commercial on the air as fast as possible. However, that was never best for the client. There needed to be time to meet, write something creative, involve them, and make magic happen. At the local stations, you were lucky to have five days for the process and you were juggling four to five productions a week. It was "wham bam, thank you ma'am." Stages Video found a great niche in delivering great customer service and creative ads.

Our next location was on Broadway Street in Myrtle Beach, just down from city hall and few years later we had saved enough to buy an old house at 514 Twenty-Ninth Avenue North in Myrtle Beach where we turned a master bedroom into master control! Twenty-five years later, we are both gainfully employed by Stages Video Productions along with Dave Conklin, who is an excellent editor and computer genius.

However, after the cancellation of "Southern Style" in 2008, I felt lost. Yes, I had a paying gig at Stages Video, but I needed an outlet for what I do best – TALK! It was the first time in my career that I did not have a radio or TV job. I felt disconnected. Chuck and I, along with an advertising friend, George Durant, decided to put together a medical show called "Thirty Minute Medical" which ran weekly on WBTW. Hospitals and physicians paid to be on, while non-profit health organizations did not. George handled sales, Chuck the production, and of course I booked the guests and conducted the interviews. We felt it we had a great product and we bought thirteen half-hour time slots on WBTW right after "Wheel of Fortune" on Saturday evenings. Yes, that was an expensive purchase. But this was in the fall of 2009, the great recession was in full swing and getting advertisers was a tough sell. We felt that if we could just get it on the air, it would sell itself. So, as soon as we had enough sponsors to cover our expenses we went on the air. But we just couldn't find enough sponsors to make it work for another thirteen weeks. We lost several thousands of dollars on that project, but it was a classy show that looked better than any of the other local shows on the air.

Thank goodness for my dear friend Matt Sedota, station manager for WEZV, better known as EASY Radio. Matt came to my rescue and offered me "Diane At Six – The Happening Hour." I love hosting it, researching, and announcing all the wonderful events and festivals around town and playing the great music of relaxation. Chuck taught me how to record and edit the show, which was a challenge for me since I have always been technically intimidated, but I'm a whiz at it now, thanks to Chuck! The EASY Radio family and listeners are the best of the best. When we sponsor an event, we pack the house with our faithful following.

In 2011, Mike Hagg, president of HTC who used to work at Cox Cable with me, asked if I was done mourning "Southern Style" after all this time. I told him I would never be done mourning "Southern Style" but I was ready for a new opportunity if he had one. He said he liked that answer. Graciously, he invited me to do whatever I thought the community needed in the way of a good wholesome TV show. This is every producer's dream, to have a chance to create something new and exciting. The only negative was that all my viewers on Time Warner would never see the show, and I had built up a fabulous following. This show would only air on HTC, but since it is one of the most respected local companies and the largest cable co-op in the country, I was thrilled, honored, and up for the challenge. Mike loved my hour-long concept of shooting on location rather than in a studio and featuring farms, food, non-profits, and everything in between. The only thing he asked is that half of the show feature east of the waterway, and the other half west of the waterway, where most of HTC customers reside.

"Inside Out" went on the air in 2012 and takes viewers inside and outside of Horry and Georgetown counties. This show has been a blessing, as I adore every single segment traveling around the area and focusing on many unknown treasures. Best of all, it was Mike's idea for Stages Video to do the production with Chuck as the director, making "Inside Out" twice as much fun. Together with my work at Stages Video Productions, EASY Radio, and HTC, my plate is full and I am happy doing all the things I love._

Another facet of my work is that I have been asked to emcee festivals, pageants, dog shows, grand openings, fundraisers, parades, male beauty pageants, speak at civic clubs, libraries, retirement homes, banquets, conventions, and fashion shows. Most of the time, there is no compensation for this. Some TV stations pay their on-air personalities a fee for representing them, but that has never been the case with me. It has all been done for the good of the organization and the community. I am sure I have done more emceeing than any other media person in town, and I'm proud of it. I charge a fee if I emcee a function for a business, but if it is non-profit, I am thrilled to help them make money.

Since I set out to be a writer, I am also fortunate to be able to write for several publications like *Sasee Magazine*, *Woman Magazine*, and *Transitions* here in Myrtle Beach, as well as other regional media. Most nights while Chuck unwinds reading, I sit in front of the computer writing.

Today I feel like one of the luckiest people in the world because I stuck to my guns, knew what I wanted to do in my career, and knew the place I wanted it to be, the Myrtle Beach area. I have been here to watch it grow and help it to grow by promoting all things culturally enriching for the community. So, as you can see, I really have been "Floating On Air."

Folks always ask me who my favorite interviews have been and I always tell them that it wasn't the celebrities at all, but rather the local guests who bared their souls to help others: Rusty, who came to talk about AIDS; Bunny, who had breast cancer and started a support group for other women; Billy, who wanted to save women's lives by talking about his wife's ovarian cancer; Harry, who could have been playing golf every day instead of trying to build a performing arts center; Marge, who dedicated her life to make Myrtle Beach a better place to live; and Merlin, who was nothing short of a hero to the citizens of North Myrtle Beach. You'll meet these outstanding personalities and many others as you turn the pages. As for the celebrities, I chose them to take the lead in the book because they will be more familiar to most readers.

Thank you for joining me in this romp through four decades of my career. I promise lots of laughs along the way and stories that I know will touch your heart as they have touched mine.

Celebrity Stories

Dolly Parton

I was young. She was young. I had big hair and she had big hair. Even though I was always well endowed, she beat me by a mile. Dolly Parton had just left Porter Wagoner when I had a chance to interview her for radio around 1975. Dolly was one of the visiting stars at the Southern 500 Race in Darlington, South Carolina, and I got the phone call to come and meet her.

Back then, things were not as easy technologically as they are now. I couldn't just pull out my iPhone! I was given a tape recorder by WOLS Radio to capture the Parton highlights, something I had never done up before and I was nervous about getting it right. Dolly was not a big star yet, but she was rising fast and I did not want to return to the radio station with nothing on tape. I was always insecure about being "technically illiterate."

I was shuffled to an area where there was a portable trailer that gets hauled behind a car, truck, or bus. I was told by Southern 500 Director Bill Kiser to stay right there, as Dolly would be returning soon. So there I stood, tape recorder in hand, anxiously awaiting Dolly.

She arrived looking gorgeous, reminding me of a heavier Ellie Mae Clampett from the "Beverly Hillbillies." Her complexion was peaches and cream and her humongous hair made her look taller than she really was.

"Hi, I'm Dolly," she said in an almost squeaky voice. "I heard you're gonna do an interview with me!"

Well, she opened the back door to her trailer and I gasped at the many blonde wigs on Styrofoam mannequin-type heads. She giggled that now-famous Dolly laugh and said "I have a wig for every day of the year! Even my husband Carl has never seen my real hair!"

We sat on two little stools set up for us inside the trailer and I knew only had ten minutes to get to know this blond bombshell performer. She was sweet and charismatic, and talked about how she hated leaving Porter, who was a true mentor to her, but she was anxious to spread her wings as a solo artist as she had been writing songs since she was a kid. "If I don't bring these songs to life, who will?" she said.

Dolly was born in Sevierville, Tennessee, the fourth of twelve children. Her father was a tobacco farmer and she grew up "dirt poor" in a rustic one-room cabin. Her "grandpaw" was a holy-roller Pentecostal preacher, and since church was a big part of her upbringing, so was music.

At nine years old she started singing on a local radio show, then TV, and when she graduated from high school, she packed up her few belongings and moved to Nashville where she first saw acclaim as a songwriter. Skeeter Davis, Kitty Wells, and Hank Williams, Jr. all sang songs written by Dolly. But her first big break as a singer was a complete flop.

In 1965, Monument records pitched her as a bubble-gum pop singer with the song, "Happy, Happy Birthday Baby," because they did not feel Dolly was the right sound for country. However, in 1966, Dolly did the harmony for Bill Phillips on his recording of a country music song, "Put It Off Until Tomorrow" that went to No. 6 on the country music charts, and Dolly, who did not even get credited on the recording, was on her way up the ladder of stardom. Her first single "Dumb Blonde" was one of the few singles that Dolly recorded but did not write.

Dolly married Carl Deen in 1966, who she had met two days after getting to Nashville at the Wishy-Washy Laundromat. He rarely travels with her and she says he is her first and last husband.

Since that interview, I have been in Dolly's company three times over the years at press conferences at the Dixie Stampede, which is now Pirate's Voyage in Myrtle Beach. At one of the media events during the question and answer period, I said "Dolly, I interviewed you in 1975, and you are more beautiful and younger looking than you were then!"

Dolly replied, "That's because I have been nipped, sucked, and tucked more than any human has the right to be." That's Dolly for ya!

THE HOLIDAY SHOW
WOLS RADIO FLORENCE, SC

Photo: complements of the Dixie Stampede

Robert Duvall

Let me set the stage. I was hosting a televised dance show at a local nightclub with five couples competing for the championship and the opportunity to return at the end of the season for the grand prize of $1,000. It was called "Studebakers Live." While I was waiting for the judges to add up their scores, I noticed some excitement stirring among the people in the audience. Robert Duvall and a good-looking woman were jitterbugging on the dance floor.

Normally I am not the kind of person who would interfere in those private moments that we all know celebrities rarely get to experience. One time while in Canada, a man asked me to take his camera and snap a picture of him and his family in front of a fountain. I recognized him right away as Michael J. Fox's dad, Michael Gross, on "Family Ties," but did not acknowledge it. We even stood and chatted for a while but I did not want to be in his face about his fame. After all, everyone deserves his or her privacy. But here was Robert Duvall, shaking a leg and seeming to enjoy the cheers from the crowds, so, tactfully as he finished dancing, I asked him if he would let me talk to him on camera as soon as we resumed the show. He said, "Of course! Would love to."

As the cameras rolled, Robert Duvall in his sloppy blue jeans, looking much younger than in his movies, chatted with me about what he was doing in our neck of the woods. He said he was making a movie in Wilmington, "Days of Thunder," and was a lover of all types of dance, and had even taken tango lessons to look better on the dance floor and attract women. Next thing you know, he fell in love with the dance and opened several tango studios. He admitted with a giggle that he had been married to several professional dancers and also said he loved our state dance, the shag, as it was so rhythmical and smooth.

For those of you who don't know who I am talking about, Robert Duvall has won Academy Awards, two Emmys, and four Golden Globes, among others. He is a writer and director as well as an actor starring in "The Godfather" Part I and II, "The Great Santini," "The Apostle," and the mini-series "Lonesome Dove," just to name a few.

After our interview, Robert hung around, gave out autographs, and continued dancing with his partner. He was just a genuine down-home guy who seemed to get a kick out of being on "Studebakers Live" even though he has been on Hollywood's greatest silver screens!

STUDEBAKERS LIVE
WCOX/ TIME WARNER CABLE
MYRTLE BEACH, SC

Mickey Spillane

It started out bad one early morning in 1982. The crew and I drove an hour and a half to get to Murrells Inlet from our WPDE TV 15 studio in Florence to meet Mickey Spillane at 8 a.m., which he said was the most beautiful time to see the rising sun reflecting on the water. No more explanation needed. I got up at 5 a.m. to get ready for this interview.

The station planned an hour-length special on Mickey, our most famous area celebrity. He was the most translated of all writers with his books published in every language imaginable, and as he said, "even pig Latin." More than 225 million of his crime novels have sold internationally and in 1980 he was recognized for having seven of the top fifteen best-selling fiction titles in the country.

Mike Hammer, his infamous private eye, was a household name and Mickey loved every second of it. So getting an interview was one thing, but having an entire day with Mickey to shoot an hour-long show was such a thrill for me even though I had never read any of his books, a fact he always teased me about.

As we arrived at Mickey's gorgeous home on the inlet, he was nowhere to be found. Even a knock on the door went unanswered. So we beeped the horn of the station van that finally got Mickey moving downstairs to open the door. I had done my due diligence and called him the day before with a reminder as I have always done for all my guests, but Mickey had partied too much the night before and was in no shape for TV cameras.

He invited us to sit down at a wooden picnic table on the property while he tried to wake up and sober up, but I knew drinking another beer as he was doing was not the answer. Plus I was shocked that it wasn't a Miller Lite, the drink Mickey touted in television commercials. After an hour of Mickey continuing to drink as he chatted with us, he still wanted to do the interview, but I refused. I told Mickey that he was in no shape to deliver his best, and I would prefer to let him off the hook as long as he promised to let me come back in a couple of days because we had already promoted and advertised the one-hour special and it had to get shot and edited.

That one single act of kindness made Mickey my biggest fan. Just ask his wife, Jane. She will tell you he admired me for not letting him go on camera and make a fool out of himself, even though the crew thought I was crazy and the boss was not going to be very happy when I got back to the studio with nothing. I swore the camera crew to secrecy. We would not embarrass Mickey. We told the boss that Mickey woke up with the flu and asked us to come back another day. And we did.

Our one-hour special was magnificent. Mickey was full of himself. He decided to give me his best since I rescued him from his worst. We talked about New Jersey, where we both were from. He was from Elizabeth, me from Newark right next door. He told me how he flew over Murrells Inlet during World War II as a pilot and said, "That is where I want to live." We talked about his past two wives, his children, and how he met Jane one day when she passed through his yard as a kid on a bike and played with his children. Mickey was just plain giddy with a sparkle in his eye when he talked about Jane, who he married the next year in 1983.

During this interview I found out that Mickey hated the word "author." He was adamant that he was a writer, and was proud to still be using a manual typewriter. He said hearing those keys click was music to his ears! He started out as a comic book writer, creating adventures for Superman, Captain Marvel, Captain America, and others. Mike Hammer started out as a comic book character called Mike Danger, but found much more fame in the pages of Mickey's crime books instead.

Mickey even had a job as a trampoline performer for Ringling Brothers Barnum & Bailey circus. And he had the most amazing success with six and half million copies of "I, the Jury" sold in our country alone, not to mention worldwide sales.

Our TV special was sensational. It ran in July during a ratings period, which is very important to TV stations. Everyone who saw it said there was a real bond between Mickey and me, which of course came from the way I handled our initial visit. At the end of the show, we even rode off into the sunset in his really cool Jaguar, a gift from John Wayne. The boss loved the show, and I got rave reviews from viewers who got a wonderful glimpse into Mickey's private life, and best of all, we won the ratings war for that time period.

Mickey was head cheerleader for the area. He loved Murrells Inlet and was proud to call it his home. I am proud to have called him my friend, and he made six more appearances with me on TV after that on my various other shows.

In 1985 I was honored to interview Mickey on Grand Strand Gazette for WBTW- TV 13. Mickey asked me if I had read any of his books yet, and I was honest and said no. He said if he were smart, he would make that a prerequisite to his allowing reporters to interview him. I replied that if I knew everything about the books and Mike Hammer, I would not have any questions! Mickey laughed and said that I was probably right.

He also turned the tables on me and during that interview and asked me why I was still here in the area when I should be in a major market. I simply said, "I am here for the same reason you are here, Mickey. I love it here. It's not about fame and fortune." That answer made him smile and snicker. It was obvious we had a mutual admiration society going.

While hosting and producing "Southern Style" for Cox Cable and Time Warner from 1985 to 2008, I had Mickey on about five times. He was always accessible to me, and as far as I know, to other local media as well. He respected us all, even though he was interviewed nationally by the biggest and best.

In August of 1987 Mickey and I were both honored for our conservation efforts by Paul Vernon, president of the South Eastern Sport Fishing Association. It was such an honor to stand arm in arm with Mickey and receive this prestigious award.

One year later, Mickey was doing a gig with Marvel Comics and called me and asked if I would like to interview Joe Sinnott while he was here in Myrtle Beach. I said, "Absolutely, but please tell me who Joe Sinnott is!" Mickey boastfully said with a hearty laugh, "He just happens to be one of the best comic artists in the business today." And so, I did, as you will read later.

On Mickey's 80th birthday I invited him to the studio for a celebration on the air. He brought Jane and we had a jab-fest. Jane and I hardly let Mickey say a word. Go figure. It was much like a roast with cake, candles, and the works. Mickey loved it.

On March 9, 2005, Jane threw a big birthday party for Mickey at their home. I was thrilled to be invited. At that time Mickey presented me with a card that I treasure and have in my jewelry box to this day. At the top it says "Hammer Investigating Agency" and below that it reads

"Honorary Doll."

Mickey died at home of pancreatic cancer July 17, 2006, at age 88. His funeral was a beautiful celebration of his incredible life with all the people he loved and who loved him. I was so grateful to be a part of it. In case you can't tell, Mickey is truly one of my favorite interviews of all time.

PEE DEE PEOPLE
WPDE-TV 15
FLORENCE, SC

GRAND STRAND GAZZETTE
WBTW-TV 13
MYRTLE BEACH, SC

SOUTHERN STYLE
TIME WARNER CABLE
MYRTLE BEACH, SC

Terry Brobst, Chuck, Mickey Spillane, and me

Coast Guard AuxillaryAwards-1987

Jimmy Carter

Hey, you've got to have confidence in yourself no matter what you do. If you do something that appears stupid, laugh along with everyone else. It isn't brain surgery. No one got hurt, right? Well that's what I keep telling myself about the day I asked Jimmy Carter, "President of what?" Was I embarrassed to have been the only journalist to ever ask Jimmy that question? Heck no, and here is why.

I was co-hosting a live radio show in Florence with my partner in crime and mentor, Doug Williams, who had been behind the microphone for twenty-five years at this time, but unfortunately neither one of us were incredibly astute in national politics.

Let me set the stage for you. This was "The Holiday Show," a live public affairs broadcast on WOLS Radio. It was Florence, South Carolina's one and only walk right in, sit right down and let's chat, hour and a half, never know what's going to happen next, program! Locals knew they could stroll into the Holiday Inn Downtown dining room, sign the guest book, and talk about anything they wanted to, within reason, of course. This was my training ground, my journalistic boot camp. It was the most-listened to radio show in the area, and the most respected as well. However, many celebrities with much bigger names graced the airwaves: Amanda Blake who was Miss Kitty on "Gunsmoke," Howard Keel of Broadway fame and later "Dallas," General William Westmoreland of the Vietnam War, and even Guy Lombardo, Mr. New Year's Eve himself, who just happened to be having breakfast one morning when we were broadcasting. But never before in the history of "The Holiday Show" had anyone announced his presidency right before our very eyes, and right before our listeners' ears!

One morning in the middle of Doug's commercial for Piggly

Wiggly, this young man, maybe 20 years old or so, walked over from where he was eating breakfast and said, "Hi, I'm Chip and I was wondering if my dad could come over and be on the show?"

"Absolutely," I said. "All he has to do is sign in and tell me what he wants to talk about."

A man dressed in deck shoes, blue jeans, and a plaid shirt approached the table, and I pointed to the chair for him to take a seat and sign his name in our little black book. About the same time, Doug finished his live commercial and turned the microphone toward me to introduce the next guest. I told Doug and the listeners that this new friend just finished having breakfast with his son here at the Holiday Inn. His name is Jimmy Carter.

"Good morning, Jimmy, and welcome to The Holiday Show," I said.

"Yes, I am Jimmy Carter and I'm running for president!"

Without skipping a beat, I asked, "President of what?"

Keep in mind: this is Florence, South Carolina. The only presidents we ever met were from Rotary, Sertoma, or Civitan clubs. But I'll never forget Jimmy Carter's answer as long as I live because he said it so proudly and boldly, "President of THESE United States."

He went on to say he was from Plains, Georgia, and had some personal business in Florence. After seeing our unusual radio format he had decided to announce his presidency right there on the spot. He said the show was real "Americana," and even though he was several months away from an official announcement, he just felt the urge to announce it right NOW.

Meanwhile, I am kicking Doug under the table as if to say, "we have a live-wire crackpot here." Part of me thought this guy must be crazy or drunk, but he was just so likable and charming with his down-home style. Doug asked him some tough questions about his goals for the future, and I followed with a few good ones of my own, like what he had been doing professionally up until this time. Needless to say, when he said he had been a "peanut farmer," I about lost all self-control and continued to ask if he had any political experience. His answer shocked both of us. He said he had been the governor for the state of Georgia.

At that point I was convinced we had been shammed, however, we continued to play the little game, giving Jimmy the respect and dignity we had always given every guest, good or bad. After the interview, Jimmy and Chip went about their business and we were left with fifteen minutes of show time, laughing between commercials and music, wondering if we had been taken for a ride.

The moment we signed off the air, Doug and I hastened to the radio station to do some research. Did Georgia ever have a Jimmy Carter as governor? Let's face it, I couldn't tell you today who is the current governor of Georgia. Could you? But to our surprise, we found out Jimmy Carter was a former governor of the Peach State. Now we asked ourselves, was this the REAL Jimmy Carter? We even called the local Democratic Party chairperson who said it was rumored that Jimmy Carter would soon be announcing his presidency, but they assured us had the REAL Jimmy Carter been in town they probably would have known about it.

About a year later, the whole world got to know that a peanut farmer from Plains, Georgia, was running on the Democratic ticket for president of THESE United States. Seeing his smiling face on national television assured us that we were not spoofed on our own radio show, but rather humbly honored by his presence and surprise announcement. We had assuredly met and interviewed the REAL Jimmy Carter.

The only part of the story that Doug and I have never agreed on is that I believe Jimmy was in Florence getting a new set of teeth, since Chip had said something to insinuate that. Let's face it, Florence use to be the "Dental Capital of the World." Senior citizens would come by the busloads to get a full set in twenty-four hours. Doug insisted that Jimmy Carter could afford teeth in Georgia if he needed them. I still believe today that he got a new set of dentures, which might explain why no one from the Democratic Party knew anything about his visit. I still laugh about the part we played in this historic event. Did I vote for Jimmy Carter? You bet I did. I followed his presidency with gusto and pride. I was one of his biggest fans.

Just a few years ago, I was in Italy vacationing with my husband when Jimmy Carter won the Nobel Peace Prize. Watching the presentation on television, knowing how much he did for our country and world peace, knowing how he fostered Habitat for Humanity, and knowing how he gave Doug and I the thrill of a lifetime, I was filled with emotion and cried like a baby for the man I came to know and admire as the REAL Jimmy Carter!

HOLIDAY SHOW
WOLS RADIO
FLORENCE, SC

This story was first published in *Sasee Magazine*,
Myrtle Beach, SC

Nancy Kerrigan

My whole family loves ice skating and ice dancing. We have followed all of the televised ice events from "Ice Capades" to "Disney on Ice," as well as all of the Olympic competitions. Therefore it was very exciting when Myrtle Beach debuted "Magic on Ice" at Fantasy Harbor in the late '90s. Thrills for me came when some of the visiting skaters came on TV to publicize the show.

Nancy Kerrigan won her first skating competition at age 9 in her hometown of Stoneham, Massachusetts. As she told me during the interview, her two older brothers played hockey but it was not appropriate at that time for girls to play, so she took skating lessons starting at age eight.

Nancy's career blossomed in the '90s as she won medals galore, but it was the physical attack by Tonya Harding and all the drama that went with it that put her even more into the spotlight. She gained a lot of support after that but lost a lot after several unfavorable comments to the media about competitors, especially Oxana Baiul. She somehow always came across as bitter rather than endearing. However, sponsors rallied around her from Seiko, Reebok, Campbell's Soup, Disney, and Evian. They loved her wholesome Irish looks, even though Nancy says that there is very little about her that is Irish, except for her name.

More controversy followed at the Disney Parade. Disney was a $2 million sponsor. Nancy was heard telling Mickey Mouse, "This whole parade thing is dumb. I hate it. This is the corniest thing I have ever done." Then in 1995, she married her manager, her first, and his third and because of this, the once-loved Kerrigan again became folly for the media.

When she came to my studio, I knew she probably would be nervous that some small-town TV host might nail her with negatives. So, when she arrived I hugged her and said, "We are only going to talk about all the positives in your career and there are many. You can lead the way, and I will follow." I assured her I was a fan. Then she thanked me and hugged me back.

The interview went great. I told Nancy I had always admired her parents who were featured many times over the years cheering from the bleachers for her. Her mom, while legally blind, was always in attendance, along with her dad who was president of her fan club. She told me her dad was her hero and bent over backward to give her the lessons she needed to succeed on the world stage. Nancy said she was genuinely thrilled to bring her talents to Myrtle Beach and maybe inspire some young girls to take up skating. I'm sure she did exactly that as "Magic on Ice" ran for several years with various ice stars strutting their stuff.

While she was in town, the Myrtle Beach Pelicans baseball team had a celebrity night where local media played against each other. Nancy was asked to play and could have said no but she came out with the rest of us in her blue jeans, T-shirt, and tennis shoes and played like a trooper. I must admit that when her second time at bat came, she asked me to fill in for her as she had a fear of being hit by the pitcher's ball. So I guess you can say I once filled in for Nancy Kerrigan. Just don't tell anyone it wasn't on the ice rink!

SOUTHERN STYLE
TIME WARNER CABLE
MYRTLE BEACH, SC

Charles Kuralt

Charles Kuralt was known and loved as a great journalist who touched the hearts of viewers with his stories from the heartland of America. His "CBS Sunday Mornings" series was tops in the ratings for many years. Fortunately for me, I was contracted to host and produce a magazine format show in the early days of the CBS affiliate in Myrtle Beach. "Grand Strand Gazette" ran on Sunday mornings after his ever-popular program. Chuck, who was the director of the show, wondered if we could solicit Charles Kuralt into doing a joint promo that would help us promote our show. Chuck wrote to the producers of "CBS Sunday Mornings" and learned that Charles would love to do it. The whole idea was that Chuck would write a piece for Charles to do in his New York studio, and I would do my part in Myrtle Beach. Through the magic of post-production, it would appear that we were in the same room doing the promo together.

We were so excited at Charles' eagerness that we sat down and created this really fun promo playing off the popularity of Prince Charles and Lady Diana. "Have Sunday Brunch with Charles and Di! 'CBS Sunday Mornings"with Charles Kuralt here on CBS followed by 'Grand Strand Gazette' with Diane DeVaughn Stokes." That was the gist of it.

Low and behold, Chuck got a call from the execs at CBS that Charles, who was from Wilmington, North Carolina, was coming to the Myrtle Beach area to speak at a convention and would gladly meet with us to do the promo in person prior to the event. One month later we were live in a banquet hall with Charles Kuralt doing our bit together – the CBS duo of Charles and Di.

Charles was warm and thanked us for coming and said he was thrilled to have been a part of it. He thought the play on the Prince and Princess of Wales was a hoot.

I had always loved "CBS Sunday Mornings" and Charles' other series, "On the Road" because feature stories, rather than hard-core news, was always my forte. Even today, if I could travel to do the same type stories that were done by Charles Kuralt, I'd jump at the chance. He has always been my favorite journalist. He could get down and dirty with the farmer and at the same time stand tall with politicians. I loved his books, his warmth, and his style.

His death in 1997 from lupus saddened his many fans, including me, and left a huge void in the CBS news team that has yet to be filled.

GRAND STRAND GAZETTE
WBTW-TV 13
MYRTLE BEACH, SC

Vanna White

I have been fortunate to be in Vanna White's presence several times over the years. She is every bit as sweet and pretty in person as she is on the air. I never got to interview her on any of my TV shows but I did get to interview her during a local press conference and at the Sun Parade when she was one of our guest celebrities.

During the press conference held in Myrtle Beach when "Wheel of Fortune" was in town recruiting contestants, Vanna was asked by one of the media how she landed the job despite all the beautiful women who applied. She said she knew the alphabet better than anyone else. No one laughed at this because they were not sure if Vanna meant it to be funny or not. I'm still not sure.

I became a Vanna fan after she appeared in the Sun Fun Parade. As she approached the reviewing stand in a red convertible, a parade volunteer handed her the microphone. She waved up to me as I spoke down to her from the upper level of the old Myrtle Beach Pavilion. I told her that her husband and children, Nickolas and Giovanna, were in good hands up there with me and would meet her here after the parade. She giggled and told them to behave and use their manners, which they did. They were both adorable.

Vanna explained how wonderful it was to be back not only in Myrtle Beach but also at the Myrtle Beach Pavilion where she spent many a night dancing, dating, and having fun. She said we might not believe it, but she misses all that was a part of her past. "Hollywood is nice, but not as nice as Myrtle Beach." That was the extent of my talk with Vanna as the parade was backing up down the boulevard.

Vanna was born and raised in North Myrtle Beach and went to North Myrtle Beach High School before heading to Atlanta to pursue modeling. Her first stint in TV came when she won a chance to be a contestant on the "Price Is Right" but did not earn a chance to make it on stage.

Then in 1982, after being one of three alternate hostesses, she got the job to serve as co-host on "Wheel of Fortune."

Vanna has since appeared in a few films, other TV shows, and authored a best-selling book, "Vanna Speaks!"

Vanna told me that many people ask her if "White" is her real name, and it is. Vanna was born to Joan and Miguel Rosich, but her father abandoned the family and she took the name White from her stepfather Herb. He worked in real estate for years in North Myrtle Beach and Vanna's mother Joan was loved and admired for her benevolent work with charities in the area. She has since passed away, but Vanna comes home regularly to visit Herb, the dad she adores.

My buddy photographer Jack Thompson, who has always had a secret crush on Vanna, was kind enough to snap a few pictures of us together at the Sun Fun Party. Two things you need to know: even with very little makeup, Vanna is still attractive and never makes herself up as a star when you see her around town. And you know how TV adds weight to just about everyone? Well, Vanna is an incredibly slim person so on TV she always looks like a Barbie doll in all those gorgeous gowns. Having never been very thin myself, this is an enviable feature of Vanna that I hope I can emulate in my next life!

PRESS CONFERENCE & SUN FUN PARADE
MYRTLE BEACH, SC

Photo: Jack Thompson

Tip O'Neil

House Speaker Tip O'Neil was a very outspoken Democrat who served thirty-four years representing Massachusetts. He was speaker of the House from 1977 to his retirement in 1987. In the late '70s he came to Florence on behalf of the Democratic Party and visited "The Holiday Show." He was big and burly, had a full head of gray hair, and a big red nose that seemed to light up when he laughed. He was also a great hugger, might I add.

He talked a little bit of politics but had more fun playing radio announcer, helping us do live radio commercials by reading the printed copy with gusto and inflection straight from his diaphragm. Tip said he was a bricklayer before he got into politics, but always wanted to do radio because he knew he had the voice for it. He also made a joke that in many ways he was still laying bricks, one at a time in Washington!

But what really made the day fun was that Lash La Rue, the mustached, whip-snapping cowboy of yesteryear, was also on the show that day. Tip had a ball asking Lash questions about the old-time Western movies and TV shows. He remembered them all, unlike me! Then the tables turned and Lash asked Tip some questions about politics. This made for lots of laughs and one of my most enjoyable days on radio. The biggest belly laugh of the day, however, came when we told him that Jimmy Carter had announced his presidency on this radio show about five years earlier. I'm not sure he believed it, but it was a true fact.

Tip got his name from a baseball player, James "TIP" O'Neil, even though his forte was basketball. He loved sports and was proud of his Irish Catholic background, especially his accomplishments in Northern Ireland crafting a peace accord.

I remember, long after his visit to the radio show, that I

saw him on TV in a cameo appearance on "Cheers." I was not surprised one bit, knowing what a real ham he was.

Tip was incredibly endearing, not only to us but also to everyone who came up asking for his autograph that morning. He died in 1994. At Tip's funeral, President Bill Clinton saluted Tip as a loyal champion of hard-working people.

HOLIDAY SHOW
WOLS RADIO
FLORENCE, SC

Dizzy Gillespie

Celebrities are wonderful to have on TV, and it's even better when you can promote it in advance to help build viewership. It's what ratings are all about. I had that opportunity with jazzman Dizzy Gillespie.

I was fortunate to have grown up in Florence and graduate from Francis Marion College, which is now Francis Marion University. That meant that everyone knew me and felt free to call me about ideas for upcoming shows. In this case, I got a call from the Public Relations Department of the college in 1983 that Dizzy Gillespie was scheduled to be on campus for a speaking engagement the following week and they wanted me to have him as a guest on my show.

First of all, Dizzy was a famous musician; secondly, he was from our coverage area, having been born in Cheraw, South Carolina; and thirdly, we used one of his jazz songs, with permission of course, as the opening music for my talk show "Pee Dee People." Interviewing Dizzy would truly be a highlight for me, I assured the college.

We made promos advertising that Dizzy would appear on the show, and ran them for four days and nights. Surely, we didn't want anyone to miss this. We even scheduled two other guests that day with the understanding that we weren't sure how much airtime we would be able to give them because when Dizzy arrived, we would have to drop everything to get him on the air, pronto. We knew he had a speaking engagement at the college prior to his arrival to us, and the college officials promised us they would have him there by 12:15 at the latest, knowing the show was live at noon and ended at 12:30.

Live at noon, we went on the air telling everyone that Dizzy was speaking at the college, which would be delivering him to us momentarily. Keep in mind, at 12:30 our show goes off the air followed by a soap opera, and you know how women feel about their soaps! There was no way the management could bump out the ABC programming!

So I interviewed one of our guests, and then went on to the second one we had standing by, and at 12:20 went to my final commercial break, keeping guest number two to help me kill time while I waited frantically for Dizzy. No one wants to be left guest-less at anytime on live TV. During the break I told the director to signal me immediately when Dizzy got there so I could get the present guest off the set tactfully, while moving Dizzy on gracefully.

One minute into our final segment I could tell that the camera girl was waving her hand and giving me a cue of sorts, but for the life of me I couldn't tell what she was trying to tell me. I had never seen this cue before, as she seemed to be squatting and grabbing her crotch simultaneously. To save time, right on the air I said, "Madam camera-woman, what are you trying to tell me?"

"Dizzy is here, but he is taking a leak," came out loud and clear for the entire world to hear.

"Well, I guess you all heard that. Dizzy will be with us after he takes a leak," I repeated, just knowing that everyone at Francis Marion would be so proud of me, their alumni extraordinaire, for making such a profound statement. I thanked the current guest, unhooked his microphone, and killed thirty seconds or so until Dizzy plummeted onto the set with a paper towel, still drying his hands from his visit to the john.

As I hooked on his microphone welcoming him to the show, Dizzy said, "Hope I didn't keep you waiting, but when a man's gotta go, a man's gotta go!"

The interview was wild. When I asked Dizzy what he was doing at Francis Marion, he said, "I heard you went to college there. Do you know what Francis Marion's nickname was?"

"I sure do. It was The Swamp Fox."

"That's right," he said. "Do you know who was 'The Gamecock?'"

"I sure do," I said. "Thomas Sumter."

"Pretty good. You must have studied hard in school. But I have one more for you. How do you spell rutabaga?"

"Gosh, Dizzy, I'm supposed to be asking the questions," I said.

"Ah ha, you can't spell it. I caught you." He was so cute and mischievous that I played along and of course, misspelled it. He laughed and spelled it correctly and told me I should have paid more attention when I was at Francis Marion. Fortunately after that, I took hold of the interview and asked him about his love of music and how it all got started. He told me about some of his idols from the early years of jazz, and how proud he was of Chuck Mangione, who like him came up the hard way to make a name for himself. He was full of himself, bubbling over with charm and personality, witty and charismatic to the hilt.

"Do you want to feel my pouches?" With that he caught me dead in my tracks.

"Maybe, depending on where they are located," I said.

"You know I have a disease named after me. Anyone who plays the trumpet and develops muscles in their cheeks has Dizzy Disease! Feel my cheeks," he said as he filled his mouth with air as if blowing on a trumpet. And so I did. They were the most powerful cheek muscles. It was like feeling the flexed arm muscle of Rambo! All I could say was, "Wow, what great pouches!"

After the show, he hung around the studio, shaking hands and giving autographs. He even posed for pictures with all the staff. My photo with Dizzy is one of my career favorites. He seemed to love the attention, unlike some famous people who seem to tire of it. That day, Dizzy stole our hearts. This musical genius was as down to earth as it comes and he was thrilled to know that his music was used as my show's theme song. He told me he was honored that we opened each day with his music!

PEE DEE PEOPLE
WPDE-TV 15
FLORENCE, SC

Lewis Grizzard

Humorist and author of twenty-five books, Lewis Grizzard was one of the funniest writers to read, but not necessarily one of the funniest people to meet. I met him during a press conference at Francis Marion University in the early '80s; he was part of a lecture program there. Lewis seemed almost out of place, somewhat nervous. Maybe he preferred writing than standing in front of ten cameras with lights blaring in his face. Who could blame him?

At the press conference he said that all of his books and stories were true. "How could I make this crap up?"

His book "My Daddy Was a Pistol, and I Am a Son of a Gun" was about his real-life experiences with his father. His parents divorced when Lewis was young, and he admits to having a frustrating relationship with his father his entire life.

Lewis gained high acclaim as a journalist. His writings were always filled with heart. Some of his best pieces include the Marshall University football team tragedy, Hank Aaron's incredible talent of hitting home runs, and his love of the South and old-fashioned values.

Lewis certainly goes down in history as having some of the funniest book titles:

"A Good Beer Joint Is Hard to Find and Other Facts Of Life"; "Don't Sit Under the Grits Tree with Anyone Else but Me"; "Don't Bend Over in the Garden Granny – You Know Them Taters Have Eyes"; "When My Love Returns from the Ladies Room Will I Be too Old to Care?"; "Elvis Is Dead and I Don't Feel too Good Myself"; "If Love Were Oil I'd Be a Quart Low"; "If I Ever Get Back to Georgia, I'm Gonna Nail My Feet to the Ground"; "Shoot Low Boys – They're Riding Shetland Ponies."

For being so incredibly witty in his books, Lewis received a lot of negative publicity for his condescending remarks toward gays and women, and for behaving badly at public events. He battled alcoholism, heart attacks, and three divorces. He hated computers, and continued to use his typewriter because he said, "When I write, I like to hear some noise."

I loved his books and admired him as a journalist. Not everyone can put "heart" on the page, so meeting Lewis at FMU that day was a thrill. He may not have had the magnetic personality I was hoping for in person, but he has it tenfold in each and every book.

PRESS CONFERENCE
FLORENCE, SC

Jerry Lewis

Jerry Lewis was born Joseph Levitch in Newark, New Jersey, in 1926. How do I know? Well, my Uncle Marty went to grammar school with him. He said Jerry was the class clown way back in the early days, a talent he developed from his father who was a vaudeville master of ceremonies. His mom played the piano for a local radio station, so Jerry was on stage often as a kid doing "shtick," as he called it, with both his parents. His father used the name Danny Lewis and Jerry started out as Joey but later changed his name to Jerry Lewis as to not get confused with comedian Joe E. Lewis and Joe Louis, the boxing champ.

Jerry Lewis' success is surely well known: comedian, actor, singer, film director, and screenwriter, to name just a few of his areas of expertise. Jerry's biggest fame, however came as sidekick to Dean Martin.

My opportunity to meet Jerry Lewis was an exciting one. I had been hosting telethons for WBTW-TV 13 in Florence since 1973, but in 1976 I was sent to Las Vegas to learn the behind-the-scenes action and better understand the new format for the Muscular Dystrophy Telethon to be held on Labor Day weekend. I was joined in Vegas by our telethon director Russell Smith and my wonderful mentor and co-host, Doug Williams. It was a super trip, as none of us had ever been to Vegas before. Meeting other telethon hosts from throughout the country was nice enough but getting to meet and work with Jerry was surely the highlight.

It was so amazing to watch Jerry do thirty-second TV promos with each of the 100 hosts. It was like an assembly line of the country's best TV talent, all nervously approaching the stage with Jerry. We had cue cards that were produced by the Vegas telethon team well outlined as to what we were to say and what Jerry was to say. But in typical Jerry Lewis fashion, he wound up ad-libbing so much of it that half the group got flustered and laughed through the entire thirty seconds. So be it – there was one chance for everyone with Jerry, so you knew you better be on your toes.

When Doug and I got our turn, the director said "three, two, one, cue" and we read our cue cards asking folks to tune-in to WBTW Labor Day weekend for the best Muscular Dystrophy Telethon ever. Isn't that right, Jerry?

With that, Jerry went into his Nutty Professor act, licking my neck, biting my ear, and running his fingers through my hair trying to crack me up. He kept repeating, "Whatever you say Diane is all right with me!"

Well, of course we aired the promo many times upon our return home and the locals loved it. I surely wish I had a copy of that today. But it was nothing short of pure talent, Jerry's ability to make every promo just a little bit different than the one before. Absolute genius.

That was the year that Jerry got his biggest telethon surprise – Dean Martin was invited by Frank Sinatra to appear on the show to boost ratings and dollars, and to make peace with Jerry after all those years for all the world to see. It was magical. I just wish I had been in Vegas, rather than in Florence, to witness it first-hand.

I continued to host the Muscular Dystrophy Telethons for WBTW until 1980. Then in 1981 through 1983, I hosted for WPDE-TV 15 as the station won the bid to carry the telethon, snatching it away from WBTW. That worked perfectly for me as I was now working full time as host and producer for talk show "Pee Dee People" on WPDE. It was a long weekend with little sleep but getting to know many of the region's MD patients was a bonus that kept me energized for the cause. Plus I had a chance through WPDE in 1983 to return to Vegas for another telethon training and another off-the-wall experience with the crown prince of comedy who sat on my lap like a puppet and mimicked everything I said.

In the early '90s, Jerry came to Myrtle Beach to play the

devil in the theatrical production of "Damn Yankees." During the show, he broke character for about fifteen minutes and went off into a typical Jerry Lewis comedy routine with excerpts from his many character creations. Once again, it was pure genius at work.

JERRY LEWIS MUSCULAR DYSTROPHY TELETHON
WBTW-TV 13
FLORENCE, SC

JERRY LEWIS TELETHON
WPDE-TV 15
FLORENCE, SC

Ronnie Milsap

Born in Robinsville, North Carolina, Ronnie Milsap was the first blind singer in the country music field who made a successful crossover into pop music. He won six Grammy awards and has forty No. 1 country music hits, third to George Strait and Conway Twitty. I loved his songs and his style, and after interviewing him I loved the man himself. He was just so likeable with a sweet flirtatious spunk, telling me (and probably every woman he met) that I was the most beautiful woman he had ever seen. I thanked him for that "blind compliment," and he laughed.

Ronnie had his own theater at the former Fantasy Harbor in Myrtle Beach, which was located off of Highway 501. At the time, the area was booming with other theaters that attracted motor coaches galore. Medieval Times, The Gatlin Brothers, Magic On Ice, The Euro Circus, and others comprised what was supposed to become a mega-entertainment complex. Fantasy Harbor was leading the way for Myrtle Beach to become another Branson, but sadly it failed in the attempt.

Here's what I learned from Ronnie in my interview with him that made him so endearing. He was born almost completely blind, abandoned by his mother, and then raised by his grandparents. During his early years, he lost the remainder of his sight and had both eyeballs surgically removed. When he was five years old, his grandparents thought it would be best to send him away to a school for the blind in Raleigh even though some people thought it was a cruel thing to do. Ronnie told me it was the right move because he learned from a young age to become totally self-sufficient. He learned if he was to make anything of himself, he had to tackle the world with the same gusto that he would have if he could see.

Ronnie loved music and at seven years old his teachers

noticed his musical abilities. Soon he was learning piano, studying classical music, and then rock 'n' roll. While in high school, Ronnie formed a rock band that led him to study music in college after he earned a full scholarship.

He released his first single in 1963 with some success, played piano for several popular singers, even Elvis, but it was Charley Pride who suggested Ronnie leave pop music behind and go back to country. In the early '70s, he started working with Charley's manager. Soon he became Charley's opening act, which boosted his fan base and record sales.

With one hit after another, Ronnie was an amazing crossover success from 1979 to the early '90s, making him one of the most beloved entertainers of all time. He won every imaginable award of merit: Male Vocalist of the Year, Album of the Year, Entertainer of the Year, Best Country Music Vocal Performance … the list goes on. He certainly became the pride of Charley Pride.

My favorite Milsap songs are "What A Difference You Made In My Life," " It Was Almost Like a Song," and "Stand By Your Woman Man." The next time he comes to town, I'm heading to the front row for the concert. Count on it!

SOUTHERN STYLE
TIME WARNER CABLE
MYRTLE BEACH, SC

Alabama & Mark Herndon

The country music southern rock band Alabama got its real start in Fort Payne, Indiana, in 1969 with its lead singer Randy Owen and his cousins Teddy Gentry and Jeff Cook. They were known as "Wildcountry." In the early '70s they settled into Myrtle Beach where they were the house band at the Bowery, playing for tips all hours of the night. In 1977 they changed their name to Alabama at a record producer's request. The name hung proudly on the wall behind them, as they played nightly at the Bowery.

My part of the story is this: In 1978, I was the director of sales and public relations for two Holiday Inns, in addition to part-time radio at WOLS, and TV at WBTW- TV 13 in Florence. One day, I got a phone call from the lounge manager of the Thunderbird Inn wondering where she could find a drummer. A band was coming up from Myrtle Beach and desperately needed one. Being connected with local theater and arts groups she figured I might know. I suggested she call local churches, the Florence Little Theater, or the symphony. Mark Herndon, an excellent drummer who was a student at my alma mater, Francis Marion University, got the gig. He was so fabulous that night that he became Alabama's permanent drummer. I had nothing to do with it, but I have always felt a connection.

Fast forward about to 1983. I had heard that Mark Herndon was back in the area for a while so I called his manager, who I went to college with, and booked him for a TV interview. Mark was simply adorable: long blonde curly locks, a winning personality, and an absolutely talented drummer who had been playing locally most of his life. His parents owned a home in Murrells Inlet, so he was local through and through. We had fun on the air reminiscing of when he was a starving musician, and he even made a crack about his mom, who still asks him every day, "When are you going to get a real job?" He said he couldn't believe he gets paid to be a drummer, and his mom can't believe it, either.

Then I opened the infamous phone lines! A female caller wanted to know if he was married. One of his old fans called from the Bowery to say howdy. Someone asked about "fitting in" with the rest of the members, since they are all related to each other, except for him. All great calls … up until this next one!

"Hello, 'Pee Dee People,' do you have a comment for Mark?" as I answered the phone.

"Alabama sucks."

Yes, that's what the caller said on LIVE TV! How could anyone say such a thing about a music group so All-American as apple pie, so hard working, and so family-oriented? They even sing about angels among us! You'd have to be a heathen to make such a statement. But that goes to show you that even heathens watched me on TV.

I couldn't imagine anything like this being said on such a wholesome show as mine, about the greatest band in the history of the South. But in trying to keep from gasping and admitting how mortified I was, all I could think to say was, "You must not be a country music lover. Maybe you prefer gospel!" Yep! That's what I said. Gospel, not Broadway, or big band, but GOSPEL. It was all I could think of at the moment. Anyway, Mark knew I was trying to just smooth it over. He's laughing hysterically, and says, "It's probably just one of the other three band members harassing me!" What a great sport Mark was and what a great comeback.

Moving onto other callers, everything was positive as we moved forward and when it was all over, Mark thanked me for having him on the show, hugged me goodbye, and signed autographs for the crew before driving back to his parents' home in Murrells Inlet.

A year later, I spotted Mark in sunglasses flipping through the CD rack at a local music store in Florence. Realizing he was probably trying to remain "incognito," I approached him quietly and whispered, "It's great to see you looking so handsome and discreet in your Foster Grants," and he replied, "After being on your show, I'm convinced that not everyone likes Alabama. I can't be too visible, you know!"

Mark Herndon is a super guy with a great sense of humor, and an unbelievable success story. He deserves every bit of it.

Over the years, I have attended many Alabama press conferences, including the one when the Alabama Theatre opened at Barefoot Landing in North Myrtle Beach. The guys are all terrific, down to earth, and super-talented ambassadors for the Myrtle Beach area. They still return to their roots and play at the Bowery when they are in town.

PEE DEE PEOPLE
WPDE-TV15
FLORENCE, SC

PRESS CONFERENCE
MYRTLE BEACH, SC

Nancy O'Dell

It does not get more beautiful than Nancy O'Dell. Just tune in to "Entertainment Tonight" and I know you'll agree that this host is a knockout. Nancy is a former "Miss South Carolina" 1987, and runner-up to both "Miss America" and "Miss USA." She was gorgeous from the time I first interviewed her in the mid-1990s as a star basketball player at Myrtle Beach High School. Even in her silky basketball shorts, tennis shoes and no make-up Nancy was a knockout!

Then during her pageant years I interviewed Nancy again, but I never knew she had an interest in journalism. Her southern accent was very heavy and had somewhat of a nasally tone. However, during the Miss South Carolina era, pageant directors and speech coaches offered her their best to take her to the top. Her wonderful parents were always there to support whatever she needed, as well.

She first landed a weekend reporter job in Myrtle Beach with WPDE TV 15. Then she progressed to Charleston and Miami, and moved to Las Vegas with her first husband. All of Myrtle Beach cheered Nancy on as she moved up the ladder of success in television, covering the Oscars, Emmy's, and Globe Awards for "Access Hollywood" and now "Entertainment Tonight."

Nancy is also an author of a book entitled "Full of Life" about the changes her body went through during pregnancy. Nancy is a spokesperson for Muscular Dystrophy Association and has done many telethons with Jerry Lewis, and is also an ambassador for ALS, a disease that took the life of her mother.

Just ask anyone who knows Nancy and they will tell you that she is as beautiful on the inside as she is on the outside. Her personality and svelte body make her the envy of women everywhere.

When I watch Nancy on national TV interviewing all those big-time celebrities, I am proud to say I interviewed her long before her glory days among the stars.

SOUTHERN STYLE
COX CABLE
MYRTLE BEACH, SC

GRAND STRAND GAZZETTE
WBTW-TV13
MYRTLE BEACH, SC

Billy Scott & The Prophets

Born Peter Pendleton in Huntington, West Virginia, in 1942, Billy Scott, formerly of The Georgia Prophets and in later years Billy Scott and the Party Prophets, was such a super guy. Not only did I follow his music in my high school and college years, but I also interviewed him and shared the stage with him on several occasions. Here is the story.

In 1968 he got his first gold record for "I Got The Fever." I loved that song and became an instant fan of the Prophets. Back in the late '60s I even came with friends to Myrtle Beach from Florence to see them live. They had the crowd in an adrenaline rush all night long. Falling into that beach music genre, the band was booked somewhere every weekend throughout the Carolinas for more than a decade.

During his new band era, Billy appeared on "Southern Style" several times to talk not only about music but also about an awards ceremony he was involved with that would salute the best of beach music, the Beach Music Association International. As we talked, Billy told me that he did not take the name "Billy Scott" until after he left the Army, but he felt it had a ring to it. I told him I thought Peter Pendleton had a ring to it too, but Billy thought it sounded like the name of a stripper from the "Peter Adonis Show."

Then in 2011 and 2012, I was honored to be asked by Dino Thompson to host the Beach Music Hall of Fame. Dino, owner of Flamingo Grill and Cagney's Restaurant in Myrtle Beach, spearheaded the project with such pizzazz. My co-host was Billy Scott. We had so much fun winging it that first event, and we seemed to bounce off each other very well. There was a script that Dino wrote, but there were lots of places to wing it and ad-lib. Billy was very nervous about this the first year because, as he said, he loves to sing on stage, but not talk. I love to talk on stage but not sing, so we were an excellent team. Our second year was even smoother. At that time in the dressing room prior to the show at Coastal Carolina University, Billy and I chatted intimately about how lucky he was to be healthy and fit when so many of his friends were battling illnesses. He told me that he battled throat cancer many years ago and was lucky to have beaten it. I reminded him that I saw him perform when I was in high school and he did not look any different, still slender, handsome and gray-less, which he admitted that only his hairdresser knew for sure! He said he was eating healthier nowadays because he wanted to be around for a while to make sure his grandchildren knew all about this type of music!

That same night, Billy talked with me about possibly helping him launch a project to bring beach music into the schools for kids to better understand what it is and where it came from. He promised to call me after the first of the year to kick it off.

Shockingly, two months later I got a call from a Sun News reporter to comment on Billy's death. I was very taken aback by this call, as I did not know that my friend Billy had passed away. The reporter said he died from pancreatic and liver cancer at his home in Charlotte. I told the reporter I would have to call him back before I could make a statement because all I wanted to do was cry. I did tell the reporter, however, that there was no way Billy knew he was ill the last time I saw him because we talked about how thankful he was for his good health.

After a phone call to a mutual friend, Harry Turner, president of the Beach Music Association, I learned that Billy had found out six weeks earlier about his terminal illness, following severe stomach pains. That was two weeks after our conversation at the Beach Music Hall of Fame.

He was such a picture of health and vitality a few weeks before, it just did not seem possible. Billy was 70 but looked 50.

There is no doubt Billy is in heaven teaching the angels and the original prophets from the Old Testament about beach music, the genre he loved and nurtured.

SOUTHERN STYLE
TIME WARNER CABLE
MYRTLE BEACH, SC

Billy Scott & The Prophets

Amanda Blake

Before she became the top saloonkeeper in TV history, she was a telephone operator! She was nicknamed "the young Greer Garson" and was inducted into the Hall of Great Western Performers at the National Cowboy and Western Heritage Museum in Oklahoma City. The beautiful, red-haired "Miss Kitty Russell" on the TV show "Gunsmoke" that ran from 1955 until 1974 made an appearance on "The Holiday Show" and I was awestruck by her elegance.

Amanda Blake arrived in Florence for an American Cancer Society benefit around 1979.

She was a two-pack-a-day smoker who had oral cancer in 1977 and afterwards made the rounds to urge folks to give up the habit before it's too late.

Her appearance in Florence was a sold-out event, and everyone loved the warm and charming actress who in her spare time fought as an animal activist, promoting no-kill animal shelter facilities throughout the country. A one-time board member of the Humane Society of the United States, Amanda helped form the Arizona Welfare League in 1971, the oldest and largest no-kill shelter in the state. She also made many trips to Africa and dedicated a lot of time and money to the Performing Animal Welfare Society, better known as PAWS.

Other than "Gunsmoke," Amanda was a featured guest on the "Match Game," "Hollywood Squares," and had an early stint on the "Red Skelton Show." Late in the '80s, she was in a couple of films before passing in 1989.

During her rather husky-voiced radio interview, she told about being an only child who was born in Buffalo, New York, raised knowing she was loved and "spoiled." She talked about her love of anything with four legs, as "they were helpless creatures put on this earth by God to be taken care of by all of us." And I was most surprised by her candor about her on-screen relationship with Matt Dillon. She joked about how Miss Kitty loved Matt and yet TV was so "virginal back then" that they could never make it obvious whether she and Matt ever consummated their relationship. She believed they "did it" every time they went though the swinging saloon doors together.

Referring to the TV shows of the late '70s, Amanda proclaimed, "We've come a long way, baby!"

Wouldn't Amanda be horrified to see the sex-filled television programs today?

HOLIDAY SHOW
WOLS RADIO
FLORENCE, SC

Tim Richmond

He was born in Ashland, Ohio, in 1955 and was one of the most handsome men I ever interviewed. Tim Richmond competed in Indy Car racing before transferring to NASCAR's Winston Cup Series. He was described as the James Dean of racing and earned the nickname "Hollywood."

The Jerry Lewis Telethon had always been carried by WBTW TV 13, the CBS affiliate, but in 1981 WPDE-TV 15 made a big splash as first full-time ABC affiliate in Florence and took on the telethon with vim and vigor. I was hosting and producing a live at noon talk show for them, "Pee Dee People," so I was the natural choice to host the telethon, not to mention I had done so for WBTW for many years before I made the switch to WPDE. Hence, I got to interview Tim Richmond through my Southern 500 contacts who promised to send him over to the telethon during the Labor Day weekend event.

Tim talked about his life as a kid growing up in a very well to do family and the many go-karts he owned that fueled his love for racing. His parents enrolled him in a military academy in Miami to get him away from the bullying he was experiencing due to his family's wealth. When he was 16 his parents bought him a Pontiac Trans Am, a speedboat, and a Piper Cherokee for his birthday that added to his zest for speed. And as a high school athlete he was such a great high hurdler and football player that the academy retired his sports jersey following graduation.

A friend of Tim's father co-owned a Sprint car and that led Tim to join the crew for Dave Shoemaker. That was the beginning of his NASCAR passion. There was no stopping Tim from beating his own race time with each and every attempt. He was one of the first drivers to use open-wheel racing, which is now the norm. He won the 1980 Indianapolis 500 Rookie of the Year award and during his eight NASCAR seasons, he had thirteen victories.

He was also cast in a bit part in the movie "Stroker Ace," and the Tom Cruise role in "Days of Thunder" was said to be based on Tim Richmond's life.

During our TV time together, Tim posed with me for photos that I still cherish, and he spent some quality time with our local muscular dystrophy patients before greeting the public with zest. One of Jerry's kids, as Jerry Lewis always called them, was David Chandler from Hartsville.

David was about eight years older than me, loved NASCAR, and was absolutely smitten with Tim Richmond. So I asked Tim to spend some quality time with David while he was at the station. Next thing I know, Tim invited David to the Southern 500 as his guest with special seats, free refreshments, and the royal treatment that David treasured until his death. Here was a gesture of kindness that was not done for publicity's sake, but rather for all the right reasons.

Tim died of AIDS in 1989 at 34 years old. The media reported ten days after his death that he acquired the disease from a relationship he had with an un-named woman. For a strong, healthy heterosexual male to die of AIDS was something new at that time. His parents were very brave to release the truth surrounding his death. In doing so they brought attention to safe-sex practices for all sexually active persons.

Who knows what records might have been set on the NASCAR tracts if Tim Richmond were here today! He might have had a heavy foot and lust for speed, but he also had a heart of gold.

JERRY LEWIS MUSCULAR DYSTROPHY TELETHON
WPDE-TV 15 MYRTLE BEACH, SC

Jerry Falwell

It was shocking that I was selected to represent all of the Myrtle Beach media to interview evangelical Southern Baptist preacher Jerry Falwell. Jerry was scheduled to make a stop in Myrtle Beach on his tour bus as he traveled the country, speaking about his favorite issues in the late '90s. He did not have time to be interviewed by everyone, so in each town, a local church affiliated with the Falwell network picked a representative to board the bus and literally ride several miles while conducting an interview, then get off and share the story with the rest of the hungry media.

Since I wasn't a hard-core newsperson, the selection of me was most amusing. I have always been known as the media person who preferred feature rather than news. I hated the hard, tough questions, and hated controversy as well. Most of all, I barely agreed with Jerry Falwell on anything. I knew God was much more forgiving and loving than Jerry Falwell ever was. Yet, when the call came in from a local minister, I felt too honored to refuse the opportunity, even though I was not a fan in the least. He said the committee voted unanimously for me to do this job knowing I would be the most respectful. How could I say no?

With my selection, I also knew that the other media folks were resentful, but so be it. If I was willing to give up my Saturday afternoon to hustle onto Jerry's bus, conduct a thirty-minute interview with him, then spend time at a news conference delivering the scoop and the video footage to other media, what the heck! I found Jerry Falwell to be guarded, controlling, and somewhat pompous. He barely answered any of my questions but chose to steer the interview in the direction he desired in order to strengthen his platform, which I found to be filled with more hate and anger than Christian love. When it was over, I regretted I was a part of the Falwell media motor tour.

Jerry Falwell founded Thomas Road Baptist Church in 1956

at age 22, serving as pastor for many years. In 1971 he founded Liberty University, a Christian liberal arts college and prior to that he founded Lynchburg Christian Academy, now Liberty Christian Academy. In 1979 he co-founded the Moral Majority and became incredibly outspoken, taking aim at rights for gays and lesbians, pro-life issues, civil rights, apartheid, labor unions, and others. Jerry died in 2007 and unfortunately some of his judgmental, hateful, and angry philosophies did not die with him.

SOUTHERN STYLE
TIME WARNER CABLE
MYRTLE BEACH, SC

General William Westmoreland

William Westmoreland was born in Spartanburg, South Carolina, and became the United States army general, commanding military operations in the Vietnam War from 1964 to 1968. His men said he was the most caring officer they had ever encountered, genuinely concerned about their welfare.

In the mid-1970s, General Westmoreland came to Francis Marion University to speak to the students and so we did a live remote, taking "The Holiday Show" on the road, which was rare. The college was filled with excitement; this was probably the biggest celebrity to ever appear up to that time in the college's history.

Doug Williams, my mentor and co-host, led the interview, asking about the war itself and whether Westmoreland ever felt like he would not win against the communist regime. The general said that he knew all along it was going to take time, patience, and confidence to come out of the war on top. He kept that spunk throughout the battles, and proudly said that the United States won every battle under his leadership.

My questions were on the softer side, of course, about good care for veterans, helping those afflicted in the war, and helping them move on with their lives after witnessing such horrific atrocities. As a teenager during those turbulent times, I had many friends who served in Vietnam, including a steady boyfriend who served two terms. Some returned without limbs, and some never returned at all. I also knew many who moved to Canada to avoid serving. I had not been a supporter of the war. My mom always said if I had been a boy and was drafted, she would have hauled me to Canada. We were not in favor of the United States' involvement in the Vietnam War. However, I realize now more than ever the sacrifice these men and women made in their service to our country. So interviewing General

William Westmoreland was no easy task for me. It brought back the bitterness and fear I felt for all my friends during the turbulent '60s and '70s.

General Westmoreland was gracious with all his answers and one could not help but have total respect for this incredible American hero. The horrible affliction of Alzheimer's ended the general's life in 2005.

HOLIDAY SHOW
WOLS RADIO
FLORENCE, SC

Phoebe Cates

Film actress Phoebe Cates is most well known for her roles in "Fast Times at Ridgemont High" and "Gremlins." She was able to break into celebrity circles rather quickly since her parents were Broadway producers and television show pioneers, and even her grandparents were in the business.

Phoebe always wanted to be a dancer. After attending Julliard, she won a scholarship to the School of American Ballet, but a knee injury caused her to seek a modeling career instead. She hated modeling, however, even though she said it paid the bills, so she decided to go into acting.

Her parents did not approve, and liked it less when she appeared nude in her first film, "Paradise."

She did admit later that it was wrong and she should never have done the film. She also refused to do any promotion for it after it was completed.

Yet we all remember how she dropped her bikini top in "Fast Times at Ridgemont High" though she admitted to having the time of her life filming those scenes. She even sang a couple of songs for some of her movie soundtracks. And what most people don't know is that she met her husband, actor Kevin Kline, while auditioning for the movie "The Big Chill" in 1983, even though she did not get the part. Meg Tilly got cast in the role instead.

The above are just a couple of facts I learned from Phoebe as she was making the 1989 movie "Shag" in North Myrtle Beach. The movie featured four teenage girls who escape from their parents' grasp for few days in 1963, and experienced life and love.

I was invited with my husband Chuck, who was my TV show director at the time, to come watch some of the filming. The scene we watched for more than two hours was short but not sweet as Phoebe kept trying to sound southern in her line delivery, but in doing so she sounded like she was saying "potty," not "party." The director kept saying, "Cut. Do it again." I'll never forget the exact words since we heard it delivered a hundred times during those two hours: "I don't want to go to Charleston and visit the goddamn colonial homes. I want to go to Myrtle Beach and party and meet boys!"

It was lucky for us that we got to interview her before taping this scene, because she was in no frame of mind to tape an interview with us after those grueling two hours. Phoebe is very pretty but not as warm and friendly as I was hoping. We felt she would have rather been somewhere else. She just did not seem to be having fun with us or with the making of the movie.

We also got to meet Anna Beth Gish, Tyrone Power, Jr., and Scott Coffey who were in the film and watched some of the other scenes being filmed with local shag dancers in Atlantic Beach. Anna Beth and Bridget Fonda also made an appearance that year at the National Shag Dance Championships, which I have hosted since 1989.

The making of this movie was a very exciting time for everyone in the area with stars wandering all over the community, and for many others it was the thrill of being able to appear in a big-time movie, or at least a movie that was big time for Myrtle Beach.

GRAND STRAND GAZETTE
WBTW-TV 13
MYRTLE BEACH, SC

Kenny Rogers

The beautiful Palace Theatre opened with a big cheer from everyone. Firstly, it was a great anchor for Broadway at the Beach. Secondly, it was gorgeous inside and out. Thirdly, it received much publicity since its majority owner was John Q. Hammons. In case that name does not ring a bell with you, he was one of the biggest developers of upscale luxury hotels and resorts at that time. What an honor that he chose to invest in Myrtle Beach with the Burroughs and Chapin Company.

The media was invited to a fabulous night of Kenny Rogers singing his heart out. There's no need to tell you about Kenny, as I am sure you are well aware of his awards and recognition in the recording and producing business. Maybe you did not know that his first major gig was with the New Christy Minstrels in 1966, and he has recorded with so many big-time singers: Dottie West, Kim Carnes, the Bee Gees, Dolly Parton, and others.

I'm sure everyone who was in attendance at the Palace grand opening will attest how shocked we all were to see Kenny looking younger, tighter, and really nothing like the old Kenny. It was very obvious that he had some extensive work done. When he sang and opened his mouth real wide, he almost looked like he was in pain. And maybe he was. Perhaps the surgery had just taken place weeks or days before. Unfortunately, one of the local radio deejays insulted him regarding the botched facelift and he refused to give individual interviews here in town after that.

Kenny sang songs of yesteryear like "The Gambler" and "Lucille," and some of his latest hits as well. He also sang songs recorded by other country artists. However, in the style he is known for, Kenny was totally entertaining. He just wasn't the warm personality on stage that I hoped for.

I did wish he chatted more during the show about his family, kids, and such but perhaps that was too painful since he has been married so many times.

My favorite part of the show was when Kenny sang my favorite of all his songs, "Yesterday When I was Young." However, with his new face, something was lost in the translation.

PRESS CONFERENCE
THE PALACE THEATRE
MYRTLE BEACH, SC

Photo: The Palace Theater

Meadowlark Lemon

Basketball player, actor, speaker, and entertainer "The Clown Prince of the Harlem Globetrotters" graced me with an interview in 1982. He was hired to speak at a banquet in Florence and I was fortunate to have him arrive early for a TV interview. My first thought was, "Boy is he TALL!" He was good-looking too, funny, and flirty, so much fun on the air. He even spun the basketball on his fingertip to humor me. Then he made me try to do it!

I remember he told me that he had more children than the old woman who lived in the shoe. He had ten. And I learned he was born in Wilmington, North Carolina. He also told me that when he left Florence he was headed to see some of his kinfolk across the border. I teased him about his old Burger King commercial which was one of the top commercials back in the '70s. Meadowlark, however did not want to talk about the past but rather the present. He was proud to be a born-again Christian. Even then, he did a little preaching on the air about "getting right with God before it's too late." He reminded us all that the present is a present!

On his way out the door, Meadowlark apologized that he forgot to bring an autographed picture, but he did grab a piece of paper off my desk and signed it for me: "To Diane with much love and happiness." I still have that special note in my scrapbook of memories.

Since then I have followed his career. Not only does he own "The Meadowlark Lemon Harlem All-Stars" comedy team of legendary players, but also he became an ordained minister in 1986 and received his Doctor of Divinity in 1988. His book, "Trust Your Next Shot: A Guide to a Life of Joy," discusses his rise to fame from the depths of poverty and prejudice. Most of all, it's filled with the love and laughter he so graciously shared with me. Medowlark was inducted into the Basketball Hall of Fame in 2003.

PEE DEE PEOPLE
WPDE-TV 15
FLORENCE, SC

Steve & Rudy Gatlin

Myrtle Beach was glowing when the Gatlin Brothers came to town to open a theater at Fantasy Harbor. They really bonded with the community and got involved with non-profits, played in local golf tournaments, and made the area their home away from home.

One of the highlights for me was singing with "Vocal Edition," a local singing ensemble that got invited to perform for all of the Gatlin Christmas shows one year. We kind of served as their backup singers for a medley of Christmas hymns dressed in our holiday finery. It was fame and no fortune on a personal level, but our choral group benefited with a nice donation to the treasury. However, all of us would have done it for nothing since it was as "big-time" as it got for us local singers.

During the Gatlin Brothers era, I had a chance to get to know Rudy and Steve. Rudy liked to talk about growing up in a musically talented family with his mom playing the piano and his dad the guitar. "There was never a quiet moment at our house!" Rudy was two-and-a-half when Larry, age six, convinced their mom to let him join his brothers and perform in a local TV talent show. The rest is history. They have performed at the White House, Ford Theater, Camp David, and on all sorts of country music TV shows.

Rudy also loved performing on Broadway. When I was cast as Annie in "Annie Get Your Gun" in our local theater, Rudy was quick to remind me that he played the lead male, Frank Butler, in that show in the big leagues. I also knew that Rudy played Curly in "Oklahoma!" and teased him during the interview about the role of a handsome young cowboy who gets the girl in the end. He laughed when I told him I played Ado Annie in "Oklahoma!" with the First Presbyterian Players when I was fifty years old and had to be the oldest one to ever play that role.

He laughed and said, "It's amazing what a good wig and make-up can do!"

At the end of the Gatlin Brothers' contract with Fantasy Harbor, Steve stayed on in Myrtle Beach. He loved it here, loved playing golf, and kept a condo here while making many trips home to see his wife and children. He also remained involved in the community and had many solo performances in local churches and such before throwing in the towel on his Myrtle Beach lifestyle.

A few years after Steve left the area, I got an interesting phone call from him asking if he could come back on my show. He wanted to talk to the viewers about something serious in his life hoping to make difference in the lives of others. Steve wanted to talk about depression.

Steve's TV interview touched my heart deeply. I felt like this was his first opportunity following his recovery to talk publicly about his illness. On the phone prior to this, he shared with me how he spiraled downward after he left Myrtle Beach and could not figure out why. But now it was time to give thanks to God and spread the word about this very misunderstood illness.

Sharing with the TV viewers his innermost thoughts and baring his soul, Steve said he had everything going for him, a wonderful wife, great kids, good career, gorgeous home, supportive parents and siblings, but he could not get a grip on why he felt so despondent all the time. Many people would say to him, "Steve you have more going for you than most folks will ever have in a lifetime, what are you so down about?" He knew they were right, which made him feel worse.

There were others who said, "How could a Christian like you not be able to pick yourself up and carry on?" Steve agreed with all of it. But he said at the time he did not understand depression like he does now. After many months of counseling, medication, and prayer, he has come to know the disease intimately and wanted the rest of the world to understand it as well. Steve believed that God now wanted him to tell the story of his own issues with depression so that folks would better sympathize and get help and medication for their loved ones coping with it.

Here is a story Steve told me that I repeat to friends whenever

I get the chance to do so. He said long after his recovery he saw a church that had a sign on its marquee that said, "You're too blessed to be depressed!" He was infuriated that a church, which obviously did not understand depression, was sending a message like this. It was the same message that so many people had said to Steve and the one thing that kept him from seeking medical attention all those years. It only made him feel guilty and more depressed.

Steve turned his car around and went back to that little church and asked the folks at the house next door if they could give him the name of the pastor. They did, and Steve called the pastor who met him at the church moments later to discuss the sign.

The sign was changed right then and there and the pastor thanked Steve for reminding him and educating him on the subject of depression. A clinically depressed person is imbalanced and needs medication, just like a person with diabetes needs insulin.

I thanked Steve for sharing his story with us and promised to pray for him. Steve added, "Prayer will always be a welcome addition to any addiction."

SOUTHERN STYLE
TIME WARNER CABLE
MYRTLE BEACH, SC

Steve Gatlin

Frank Abignale, Jr.

Frank Abignale, Jr. may not ring a bell to you but his famous book and movie "Catch Me If You Can" surely commands your attention.

Around 1982 Frank came to Florence to do a seminar on bank fraud and forgery and I had a wonderful experience interviewing him. At the time I did not know anything about him. He was very tall, distinguished, and had a great personality, as he said: "a perfect con-man."

Frank became one of the nation's most famous imposters. He billed himself as a doctor, lawyer, prison agent, and even an airline pilot. He also was a great escape artist, fleeing from police custody twice before he was twenty-one years old: one time from an airplane that was in taxiing mode, and another instance when he broke out of a prison. Another thing he liked to brag about was that he was one of the world's best check forgers, which led to his Florence visit.

During his time with me on TV, I was shocked to learn that Frank had spent six months in a French prison, six months in a Swedish prison, and four years in a U.S. prison. He admitted that his first con was against his father's credit card when Frank was only fifteen years old. Later he created various identities and opened up checking accounts in different names. He also claims to have created his own business checks and brought them to area banks where they would advance the money before realizing there was no such business.

I was most amazed that this seemingly sweet guy once bought a cop costume at a Halloween shop and put an "out of order" sign on an airport drop box, directing depositors to give the money to the police officer in attendance, which everyone did, making Frank a very happy man!

Another of Frank's cons was telling Pan Am Airlines that

he had lost his uniform and badge and they gave him another without question. He flew more than 250 flights to 26 countries as a guest pilot and charged food and lodging back to the company on his forged ID. The list goes on.

One of the most interesting things Frank told me was that after he served prison time, he wanted to go straight, but it was boring. There was no adrenaline rush to be a goody-goody. The really great companies were afraid to hire him once they knew of his prison record. That's when he decided to offer his expertise to banks and industries that could benefit from understanding the cons, and he in turn could make money from the presentation. That's how Abignale & Associates was born, and believe it or not, the FBI is one his biggest accounts.

Frank now lives in Charleston and must have been thrilled that Leonardo DiCaprio played him in the movie "Catch Me If You Can." Frank himself was also in the movie as a French police officer that takes the star into custody. Having seen the movie, it was simply amazing what Frank Abignale, Jr. got away with. The 2011 Broadway musical of the same name won four Tony awards.

Before he left the studio, Frank invited me to the upcoming bank seminar and I accepted. It was one of the most intriguing nights of my life realizing how naïve and trusting most people are, including myself. Frank laughed at seeing how many people at the event knew me and welcomed me with open arms. I would make the most incredible con-woman, he said, because folks believed in me and trusted me. Giving me his card, he invited me to call him in case I was ever interested in getting into the business! No kidding!

PEE DEE PEOPLE
WPDE-TV 15
FLORENCE, SC

John Davidson

From the first time I saw John Davidson on TV when I was a kid, I thought he was just adorable. Then again, I have always been partial to dimples! I used to love to watch him on "That's Incredible," "Hollywood Squares," and "The $100,000 Pyramid." I tried to never miss a variety show that he made an appearance on like "Sonny and Cher Comedy Hour," "The Tonight Show," "The Ed Sullivan Show," etc. This guy was not only funny, but he could sing.

It was around 1996 or 1997 that John came to Myrtle Beach to appear in the Broadway Musical "State Fair." I attended the press conference and was elated to meet him and have my photo taken with him. There I learned he started out as an underwear model for the Sears catalog! I was also thrilled to find out we had the same birthday, December 13, except he is ten years older than me. His parents were both ministers and John claimed he had an amazing childhood growing up in Pittsburgh. And even though he was now touring with "State Fair," "The Music Man" was his favorite Broadway show.

The production of "State Fair" was fabulous. The sets, the costumes, and the cast made the audience feel like we were on Broadway. It was so family-oriented and so bright and breezy. I was so infatuated watching John Davidson that I don't even remember whom the leading lady was. What a joy to finally meet and interview someone I had long admired and find him be even better than I expected.

SOUTHERN STYLE
TIME WARNER CABLE
MYRTLE BEACH, SC

Bobby Richardson

Direct from his hometown of Sumter, South Carolina, Bobby Richardson came to talk about baseball. He was making an appearance in Florence on behalf of the Fellowship of Christian Athletes, as he was currently the baseball coach for the University of South Carolina Gamecocks. He was simply charismatic, looking much younger than his years, and incredibly charming.

Bobby was most known as the second baseman for the New York Yankees from 1955-66. He was the only World Series player to be named "Most Valuable Player" from the losing team, a fact he was very proud about but not in a conceited way. Bobby was very humble about his talent and gave God all the glory. The number "1" on his jersey represented the person who was No. 1 in his life: God.

Not only was Bobby a great baseball player, but he was also a great humanitarian who made speeches worldwide for the betterment of the world. He was sought out as a national speaker, even preaching at the White House for President Richard Nixon.

Bobby came to "The Holiday Show" several times during the years I co-hosted. Whenever he was in the area making a speech he would just pop in, have coffee, and chat on our live microphone, and in 1976 Bobby came to talk about his run for Congress, which he sadly lost. A few years later he coached at Liberty University.

Over the years I have run into Bobby many times, especially when he was at Coastal Carolina University as head baseball coach from 1985-86. He wrote a book in 2012 called "Impact Player," detailing his career with the Yankees. You could look the world over and never find a nicer, more humble guy than Bobby Richardson.

HOLIDAY SHOW WOLS RADIO
FLORENCE, SC

Casey Kasem

I did not get to interview Casey Kasem, but I did get to pose with him and chat behind the scenes while I was in Las Vegas training for The Jerry Lewis Muscular Dystrophy Telethon.

During this rigorous three days, all the hosts from local TV stations throughout the country gathered in Vegas to learn about the telethon, about muscular dystrophy, and how our local stations tied into the big event. While the world watched the national telethon, local stations had the chance to break away from the national event and host ten-minute segments each hour that featured local patients, local fundraisers, and local entertainment.

On one of our Las Vegas mornings, we were herded like cattle into a conference room at Caesar's Palace to produce promotional commercials to air back home that featured Jerry Lewis.

However, while we were waiting for our turn up at bat with Jerry, we were divided into various groups to have photos made with a telethon celebrity. I lucked up and got Casey, who I listened to religiously on "American Top 40" each week. What a thrill! Most people got to take one photo, but Casey would not let me go, and he kept saying, "Let's do another" and so I have three photos with him and signed by him.

Casey's career began in Flint, Michigan, working as a DJ in the Armed Forces. Combine that with his love of trivia and his smoother than silk vocal cords and you can see why Casey's many radio shows have all been hits: "Casey's Top 40," "Casey's Hot 20," and "Casey's Countdown," among others. He has done a ton of voiceover work for cartoons, commercials, and movies, and even starred in a few TV shows and movies along the way.

At the end of our brief time together in Vegas, Casey made me giggle when looked me in the eye and delivered the line he ended each of his shows with: "Diane, keep your feet on the ground, and keep reaching for the stars."

Casey suffered from Parkinson's disease in his later years. He was also caught up in a bitter struggle between his second wife and the children from his first marriage. He died in June 2014.

JERRY LEWIS MUSCULAR DYSTROPHY
TELETHON WBTW-TV 13
FLORENCE, SC

Cale Yarborough

It was a big day for me. I had just met Dolly Parton and got to interview her in her wig-filled trailer when I also got a quick radio interview with Cale Yarborough, Florence's local hometown NASCAR star.

Cale was born in Sardis, South Carolina, a hole-in-the-wall community near Timmonsville, outside of Florence and was dearly loved by everyone. In high school he played football and was on the boxing team, and attended the second Southern 500 in 1951, sneaking in without a ticket. A few years later he entered the competition but was disqualified when the officials caught him lying about his age. In 1957 however, he made it in legitimately and there was no turning back for Cale. This is what he was made to do. His record is legendary. Still today folks buy cars from Cale Yarborough Honda in Florence just to feel the kinship. But it isn't Cale's outstanding racing record that I want to talk about. It's a different kind of record!

In 1979, Cale turned 40 and wanted something unique for his big birthday bash. At the time, I was dating a musician, Windy Greene, and Cale asked him if he would write a song to be sung in honor of his 40th. Windy and I had written several songs together, but this was a challenge writing for a big NASCAR star like Cale. Being the lyricist, I toyed with all kinds of spins on Cale's vivacious spirit with fast cars on the track, and in doing so I realized that there was another car that Cale was famous for, and that was his "Camouflage Cadillac." Hence the name of the song that tells of Cale's favorite way to deer hunt. Sitting in his Cadillac painted camo-style, waiting for the deer to come snooping around, Cale would roll down the window and shoot. All the folks in the area knew of his hunting escapades.

Cale loved that song so much, he sent Windy to the studio to record the song and had hundreds of 45s made to give out to all his friends, and even sold them at the Hardee's restaurants he owned in Florence. Needless to say, it got tons of airplay on local radio stations and I have to admit, it is a catchy tune with very funny lyrics.

Now here's another part of that story. Fast-forward ten years. I get a phone call from Jeff Roberts at Sounds Familiar Music Shop. Jeff was the music wizard. Folks came from all over to ask Jeff questions about music facts and artists. Jeff tells me that there is a man standing in his shop at this very minute who says there is some woman in Myrtle Beach who works in TV who wrote a song about Cale Yarborough several years ago and being a collector of Cale memorabilia, he would pay anything for a copy of that record. Did I know who that might be? Well, of course I laughed.

"It's me, Jeff."

He said, "No, really?"

"Tell the man that this is my first-ever request, and I'll be there in thirty minutes to bring him a complimentary copy as I have several left over from the original production."

When I got there, the man wanted me to sign the jacket. He was thrilled, and Jeff was too as his Sherlock Holmes effort scored him a win.

Cale is married to Betty Jo and they have three daughters. They still live in Sardis outside Timmonsville. He is a great guy, with not only a winning NASCAR record, but a winning personality as well. Here are the lyrics of the song I wrote for Cale.

"Camouflage Cadillac"
Cale Yarbrough is a good-ole boy from Timmonsville, South Carolina.
All the folks around town agree there ain't a man no finer.
He's one of racings greatest, known on every track,
But the car that Cale's most famous for is his Camouflage Cadillac.
(Refrain)
It's a Camouflage Cadillac, painted green and black.
The car that Cale's most famous for is his Camouflage Cadillac.

It fools the best of dove and quail, so the story goes.
Cale can sit there in his car without getting cold!
And when the deer run past him, they never blink an eye.
The window slowly opens- BANG- on the ground they lie!
(Refrain)
Now friends they come from far and near to hunt and fish with Cale.
Roy Clark and even Grandpa Jones can vouch for all these tales.
So if you think I'm lying, and handing you some slack,
Check out the woods around Timmonsville for Cale's Camouflage
Cadillac!
(Refrain)

It never made the top 40, but it sure was fun producing
this for Cale.

HOLIDAY SHOW
WOLS RADIO
FLORENCE, SC

Kelly Tilghman

Well, it was what you call a quickie interview. It happened during a Sun Parade rather than on TV. I was emceeing the parade as I did for eighteen years from up above at the old Myrtle Beach Pavilion as the crowds below cheered for each float or convertible that slowly approached the reviewing stand. How exciting that Kelly Tilghman, sports anchor with ESPN, had come home to celebrate all the glory that is Myrtle Beach. Her mom and dad were up top with me and I found it funny that I had interviewed them both over the years long before Kelly's own fame. Kelly's dad, Phil, was once the mayor of North Myrtle Beach where Kelly was raised. Her mom, Kathryn, is a well-known community activist and media specialist who has always fought one cause or another in order to make the area a better place to live.

As I looked down to Kelly on the street, I asked her if it was fun being in a parade that she attended all those years growing up. She said she use to like to ride in the convertible with her dad when he was mayor and made appearances in parades around town. She said, however, this was better! Kelly stressed how nice it was to be home and welcomed with such love and affection.

Thanks to Jack Thompson, I got to pose with Kelly after the parade for a glamour shot, as Jack called it!

The area is certainly proud of Kelly's achievements and her rise to fame. As a broadcaster for the Golf Channel and the first female lead golf announcer for the PGA Tour, Kelly is a force to be reckoned with. She played golf at Duke University and toured Asia, Europe, and Australia as a touring professional and teaching pro prior to her fame and fortune on the air.

Kelly is proud of her North Myrtle Beach roots and the

many golf courses in the area that have given her an incredible edge in the business.

SUN FUN PARADE
MYRTLE BEACH, SC

Photo: Jack Thompson

Guy Lombardo

Since "The Holiday Show" was live from the Holiday Inn dining room in Florence, South Carolina, you never knew who would show up.

Back in the early '70s, while ad-libbing a commercial for Rainwater's Furniture, I noticed a familiar face having breakfast. Could it really be the man who became synonymous with New Year's Eve and "Auld Lang Syne?" You bet it was: Guy Lombardo in the flesh.

I waited for he and his friend to finish eating breakfast and then ventured over to his table and told him we were doing a live radio show and would love five minutes of his time to say hello to our listeners. "Absolutely, would love to," he said.

What a jewel. He stayed for twenty minutes and discussed the big band days gone by and the wonderful musicians he had come to know over the years. He never dreamed his career would be filled with such wanderlust of travel, beautiful places, exquisite hotels, and ballrooms. He always loved music and felt grateful that a career in the business became his whole life.

He was a Canadian-American bandleader who formed the Royal Canadians back in 1924 with his brothers and other musical enthusiasts. Guy was a violinist in the early days but loved dance music, so it was no wonder he gravitated toward the upbeat tempo. He and his band became a fixture at the Roosevelt Hotel Grill in New York and later at the Waldof-Astoria. With more than 300 songs, Guy rang in forty-eight New Year's Eves from 1929 through 1976 on radio and later on TV.

Guy told us about his father, who was a great lover of music, and his mom, who encouraged both him and his little brothers to play their instruments at birthday parties and for every relative who showed up at the house. They never believed the boys could make a living doing it. One of Guy's biggest goals was to always

deliver 100 percent, giving his customers their money's worth.
And as we all know, he did.

He also gave us at WOLS Radio 100 percent by granting the
interview and sharing his personal story with us. What a treat!

THE HOLIDAY SHOW
WOLS RADIO
FLORENCE, SC

Ronald McNair

The most popular question asked of television talk show hosts is "who was your favorite TV interview"? Well, after more than forty years in the business, I have had my share of memorable guests, but the one that touched my heart the most was astronaut Ronald McNair.

Returning to his hometown of Lake City, South Carolina, where the community was recognizing him with the naming of the "Ronald McNair Boulevard" prior to his second mission into space, I was honored to land an interview with this charming and handsome man. Having been the second African-American in space, he was a hero to many. Yet it is what I found out during that interview that made him a hero to me.

Ronald McNair conquered all the odds to reach his goal. He told me as a child growing up poor in Lake City, he loved science and would sneak into the corner drug store after school and sit on the floor near the magazine rack and read Popular Science Magazine from cover to cover. His passion was outer space, and he was afraid to tell too many people about it in fear they would laugh. But the pharmacist noticed Ronald's regular visits and befriended this little boy. He asked Ronald if he would like for him to check out some science books from the local library for him to read. African-Americans were still not allowed in the library due to segregation. However, this Jewish pharmacist said he understood the prejudices of the area and had experienced some of it too, so he took Ronald under his wing and fostered his interest in science and space exploration by providing him with books to read on a regular basis. I asked Ronald about the other people who made a difference in his life and he praised his teachers and church family for nurturing his spirit, and his parents for assuring him that he could become anything he wanted to be if he studied hard enough to make it happen.

"Don't you ever worry that something could go wrong up there?" I asked Ronald during the twenty-minute live interview. Without skipping a beat, he said, "Yes, but it's what I love and worked so hard to achieve. My dream of going into space has already come true. This second trip will be a bonus!"

A brilliant student, Ronald went on to college, receiving scholarship after scholarship, getting one degree after another, not allowing anything to stand in the way of his dreams. But unfortunately, Ronald McNair, attempting his second adventure into the skies, was killed with all the other astronauts on board when the space shuttle Challenger exploded upon takeoff, as the whole world watched and cried in disbelief in 1986. It was at that moment I pledged to tell the Ronald McNair story everywhere that I could, whenever I could.

That night, I told my husband, Chuck, a video producer at the time for WBTW, what I had learned when interviewing Ronald a year earlier, including the support and friendship Ronald received from the pharmacist. Within two weeks, Chuck located and interviewed teachers, college professors, and friends, and yes, even the pharmacist who was now living in Hollywood, South Carolina, who would all be featured in a TV documentary on Ronald McNair's early life. The piece was poignant and inspiring, and the pharmacist was humbled that he helped to mold the future astronaut. The documentary was entered by former Congressmen Robin Tallon into the Library of Congress.

I have told the Ronald McNair story to the Ronald McNair Science Club at Coastal Carolina University, at career seminars in the local schools, at church gatherings, and at civic clubs. I tell it to anyone who will listen, and I tell it to YOU today. It's about determination. It's about inspiration. It's the story of working hard to achieve your goals and being touched by angels along life's path, like the pharmacist, who helped Ronald.

This beautiful success story must be told again and again. If Ronald McNair could "soar to greatness" and conquer the odds to make his dreams come true, what's stopping you?

PEE DEE PEOPLE
WPDE-TV 15
FLORENCE, SC
First published in Sasee Magazine

Ted Neely

I never thought that Ted Neely's appearance at the TV station was going to cause such a stir. Surely I was excited that I was getting an interview with him, as I was a fan of his portrayal of Jesus in Andrew Lloyd Webber's "Jesus Christ Superstar" ever since I first saw excerpts of it on TV when I was in college. The beautiful music from this Broadway rock opera permeated the radio throughout the '70s as well, even though it was very controversial at the time.

Ted was small in frame but very handsome in a rustic sort of way. He told me he had originally auditioned for the Judas role, but when that went to Ben Vereen, he signed on for the chorus and became the Jesus understudy. However, each time he took to the stage as Jesus, the audiences loved him. After many standing ovations, he was given the title role in the Los Angeles production early in the tour.

From 1992 to 1997, Ted reprised the role more than 1,700 times, having performed it for twenty years prior. He was also Jesus in the movie version. But I had no idea that so many people would recognize him when he walked into the studio.

The staff, male and female, went nuts. Some recognized him from appearing on "The Smothers Brothers Comedy Hour," "Starsky and Hutch," and the movie "Of Mice and Men."

He also played the role of Billy Shears in "Sgt. Pepper's Lonely Hearts Club Band," he was the original Tommy in the Broadway hit musical of the same name, and starred in the Broadway and LA version of "Hair." I only knew him from "Superstar." I did not expect this kind of excitement from the production team, sales staff, and front office assistants.

Ted talked about the negative reaction from churches in the early days that thought this might drive kids away from their faith, but it had the opposite effect. Many young people learned about Jesus and His teachings from this amazing theatrical masterpiece. He seemed very proud of bringing this awareness to the youth of the world.

Today it's been more than forty years and Ted Neely still brings this message to those who follow his "Little Big Band" tour, as he continues to sing the songs he once made famous as Jesus in "Superstar." He also had a cameo appearance recently in "Django Unchained," where one of his musical tracks was used.

When our interview was over he gave me complimentary tickets to the show, which was awesome, and offered all our employees an autographed picture of himself as Jesus. On my last day at the Time Warner studio, my autographed photo was still hanging proudly on my wall of fame.

Ted Neely is certainly a Broadway legend and a "superstar."

SOUTHERN STYLE
TIME WARNER CABLE
MYRTLE BEACH, SC

The Radio City Rockettes

What a glorious Christmas season when the Rockettes played Myrtle Beach. We were all so blessed to have these gorgeous, leggy young women in our community. Not only did they perform here for a couple of years, they still have many troupes rehearsing here to this day in some of the vacant retail spaces at the former Outlet Park.

As a kid growing up in New Jersey, it was the highlight of my year going to New York City for my birthday to see the Radio City Rockettes. They took the house down with every single performance back then as they continue to do today. That toy soldier number where they slowly fall one by one is still one of the best and oldest numbers in this magnificent show.

During their days of performing in Myrtle Beach, I had many Rockettes on the show, each and every one more beautiful than the next. My favorite was Linda Berres Kilponen who sent me Christmas cards for several years after her appearance. She talked about the experience of being a Rockette and seemed like a giddy child in doing so. She said she never takes it for granted as it was always a dream to dance with the best and now she was one of them.

Locally, Haley Benik of Myrtle Beach also became a Rockette and all of us in theatrical circles were thrilled since Haley had performed in many dance sequences around town over the years.

One of my biggest TV thrills ever was being invited to the Palace Theater to tape five shows with the Rockettes that would air the first week of December. In each of my tapings, I got to show our viewers a sneak peek into the "underworld" of the Rockettes. I did a segment with the costume mistress who displayed all their gorgeous array of finery. I did another segment with the seamstress who made the costumes with pieces of Velcro for easy access in and out, and also with the dance captain who explained the rigid rehearsal schedule. I asked if the women had to avoid eating certain things, and she said, "No way. When you work this hard you can eat anything you want!" I said, "Sign me up!"

The most incredible of my Rockettes adventures was when they dressed me up as a ragdoll, makeup and all. I taped my show dressed like that and interviewed two other Rockettes dressed as ragdolls also. After the interview, the Rockettes gave me a small stuffed ragdoll and a Radio City Christmas ornament as a memento. To this day, they both come out every Christmas to remind me of the day I got to be a Rockette for thirty very proud minutes!

SOUTHERN STYLE
TIME WARNER CABLE
MYRTLE BEACH, SC

**That's me as Raggedy Ann - on the left.
The Palace Theater**

Bob and Elizabeth Dole

The Jerry Lewis Telethon was a big happening in Florence each year as folks got a chance to see television at work and get to be on TV as they tossed money in buckets for this worthy cause. The fact that it took place on Labor Day weekend during The Southern 500 did not hurt one single bit. Most of the time it was just ordinary citizens making the long trek to the TV station, but every now and then, some celebrity would grace us with their presence.

I have never been a fan of politics, but the Republican Party called our director and said they were bringing out some distinguished guests around 3 p.m. to make a donation. They requested some airtime, so we waited, not knowing exactly who would show up. All we knew was that these folks were in town for the race.

Well, thank goodness the head of the local chapter of the Republican Party led the way and introduced the guests to us because I would have never known who they were. Bob and Elizabeth Dole were not known as well in the '70s as they are now. Both were very lovely, likeable, and very approachable as other contributors gathered at the station and wanted to meet them. I guess in the world of politics, any public exposure can land you a lot of votes in the future. We were fortunate they used this venue as that opportunity.

From then on, I followed both of their careers with gusto and felt honored to have met one of the most handsome and distinguished political couples of our time.

JERRY LEWIS MUSCULAR DYSTROPHY
WBTW-TV 13
FLORENCE, SC

Charles Napier

One day I got a call from BJ Thomas, not the singer but the one who owned a dress shop in downtown Myrtle Beach, and she said her niece Dee and her husband were coming to town for a visit and would I like to have him on TV. So I asked her who he was and what did he do? BJ said he was one of the men who provided growls for the "The Incredible Hulk" but had done a ton of tough-guy acting roles and that I would surely recognize him. She also said he was a great mixed media artist and had sold many of his paintings around Hollywood. So I thought, why not invite him to join me?

Born in Kentucky, Charles first became a teacher and coach, worked for a bridge company and also went into advertising before moving to Clearwater, Florida, to teach art, which was his passion.

In 1964, he went back to graduate school in Kentucky and one of his teachers encouraged him to get involved in acting at the local community theater. Eventually Charles moved back to Clearwater and became the live-in caretaker for the little theatre, where his love of acting flourished, along with his love of painting.

His big break came in 1973 when Alfred Hitchcock put him under contract with Universal Studios after seeing him in a trucker movie. At the time, he was sleeping in his car in Hollywood trying to get work. Charles also once posed as a bodyguard for his girlfriend in order to get in front of a movie producer that she knew. He told me, "Where there's a will, there is a way!"

"Star Trek" fans all recognize him from his continuous role in that series, but "Silence of the Lambs" and "Rambo" featured his most famous roles. I recognized him right off the bat! Tall, hunky, rustic, and great cowboy material, Charles was so much fun on the air. He talked about his early days before show business and how his wife Dee, the new love of his life, made him feel like a teenager again.

He also brought in ten of his unique watercolors that featured trees outlined in ink and then dribbled with color. I proudly have two of them hanging on the wall of my bedroom today. Charles died in 2011 at seventy-five years old.

SOUTHERN STYLE
TIME WARNER CABLE
MYRTLE BEACH, SC

Chuck, me, Charles Napier and his wife Dee.
Photo: B.J. Thomas

Barry Williams

I was a "Brady Bunch" fan, even though I was much older than the screaming chicks who drooled over Greg Brady, whose real name is Barry Williams. I was really disappointed when he came to the studio with a chip on his shoulder. To this day, I am not sure what set him off. It could have been that he had to find the TV studio by himself, when usually a marketing rep from the Palace Theatre would have come with him. He made some sarcastic remark that our big blue building located behind Time Warner Cable, which I admit looked like a garage, was incredibly hard to find. And the next thing out of his mouth after that was, "And do not ask me if I slept with any of my fellow actors on the 'Brady Bunch' 'cause I will totally ignore the question!" That seemed to be what all the news media want to know about – kissing Florence Henderson and dating Maureen McCormick who played Marcia Brady on the show.

To that I replied, "Well now, that we have that out of the way, let me tell you what I wish to talk about," then the cameras rolled.

I introduced Barry and asked him about the upcoming show called "Pizzazz" debuting at the Palace Theatre. Barry seemed to be frustrated that rehearsals were not going well and "You Light Up My Life" singer Debby Boone was not arriving for a few more days. It's odd that he would admit that on TV, but he just did not seem happy about anything with the show, so I changed the subject and asked him what he had been doing since "The Brady Bunch" in 1974. He told of his Broadway appearances in "Grease," "The Sound Of Music," and "West Side Story." He also had a stint on "General Hospital" in 1984.

Frankly, I was just as anxious to get him off the set, as he was to escape from the interview. He just did not want to be there, but it is usually in the star's contract to make local appearances.

I am sure he begrudged it.

As for the "Pizzazz" production – yikes! The show was a musical review of song and dance with Debby and Barry as the stars, but sadly the show flopped. Debby was awesome. She could just stand there and exude charisma. Barry was sweating bullets as he tried to maneuver through the choreography. They did not click as a team, and he never appeared to be having fun up there on stage. The audience loved Debby and no doubt Barry resented it night after night. The show only lasted one summer. There was absolutely no pizzazz there.

Today, Barry lives and works in Branson, Missouri, in another song and dance show. I hope the local media there got a better reception from Barry than I did.

SOUTHERN STYLE
TIME WARNER CABLE
MYRTLE BEACH, SC

Mark Derwin and Tom Eplin

"Soaps Alive" is an organization that sends soap opera stars into communities where women of all ages act like maniacs, screaming at their favorite daytime hotties. In August of 1991, Tom Eplin, who at the time was Jake McKinnon on NBC's "Another World," and Mark Derwin, A.C. Mallet on CBS's "Guiding Light," came to Outlet Park for an hour-long question and answer period, followed by an autograph session.

Mark was gorgeous and hunky, with eyes that would melt the coldest of hearts. When he arrived from the airport with his representative from "Soaps Alive," he threw his arms around me and said, "Kim, my God, no one told me you were going to be here." Loving the hug but confused by the statement, I said, "Hi, I'm Diane, the host for this event." He stood back, looked at me strangely, laughed, and said, "You look exactly like Kim Zimmer, 'Reva,' who stars with me on 'Guiding Light.' Oh, my God, you are a dead ringer for her."

Well, what is funny about that is that I have been mistaken a ton of times over the years as Reva Shane. I don't even watch the soaps, but I once had to turn on "The Guiding Light" just to see what this lady looked like. There is a resemblance, but surely not as much as Mark seemed to think. He could not stop talking about it. When he got out in front of the crowd he even told them how he mistook me for Kim Zimmer and asked the crowd if they agreed. And they did.

Once when I was in a mall and was approached by a woman who asked me if I was going to marry Josh after I had the baby? When I said I was not Reva she said she understood that I probably needed to remain incognito for privacy purposes! She refused to believe that I wasn't the star.

Another time I was swarmed by girls at the airport who also thought I was Reva. But here was a man who worked with her every day, and he found it very uncanny that we looked like twins, as he called it. Tom Eplin, who knew Kim Zimmer, agreed totally.

I have since seen Mark Derwin on several TV shows. A few years ago he appeared as Bonnie Hunt's husband on "Life With Bonnie," and he was featured on "Hot In Cleveland" and "How I Met Your Mother," to name a few of his acting gigs. After "The Guiding Light," he went onto the ABC Soap "One Life To Live" through 2008.

As for Tom Eplin, who also wowed the crowd that day with his baby-face good looks, he continued with "Another World" and "As the World Turns" as the same character, Jake McKinnon, for more than two decades.

I have two precious autographed photos from that day. Tom's is signed, "All My Love, Tom." Mark's says, "Diane, in my eyes you are Reva. Love Mark."

What a thrill to have spent the afternoon with these two handsome guys, pretending to know something about soaps!

SOAPS ALIVE
PRESS EVENT
MYRTLE BEACH, SC

Mark Derwin

Tom Eplin

Charley Pride

Oh, how I hated that I did not get an interview with Charley Pride. I guess I am just lucky to have met him. It was the early '70s and every day when I finished co-hosting "The Holiday Show" at the Holiday Inn Downtown I ventured upstairs to my office where the second part of my daily job took place as the director of sales and public relations for the two Florence Holiday Inns.

Within thirty minutes of finishing the live show that day, Charley Pride walked into the dining room to be on the air. He thought the show was live until noon, when we actually wrapped it up each day at eleven. The dining staff was all excited. They called me to come down from my office and meet Charley, who was having lunch with his manager when I arrived.

Surrounded by employees and other dining room and hotel guests, Charley was drawing quite a crowd. When I suggested they let him enjoy his meal, he said to me, with his sweet southern drawl, "Honey, these are the folks who made me what I am. When they stop caring, I'm in big trouble. Without them, I'd have neither fortune nor fame." It's a quote I will never forget. We all know these stars get bombarded everywhere they go. Charley's attitude must have made him weary at times. On this day, he bathed in the attention and said he would not leave until every last one of them had his autograph. It meant the world to him.

He promised if he was ever back in Florence he would return to see us and be on the radio show. Sadly, that never happened. But I am thrilled to have met this humble man who respected the fans who made him a star. In case you don't know, Charley was one of eleven children who grew up in a poor family of sharecroppers. He learned to play the guitar at an early age, but his biggest love was baseball. He played in many minor leagues, but an injury ruined his fastball. After serving two years in the military, he tried to re-gain his baseball career but realized he could not compete.

In 1965 Charley started pursuing a singing career. It was Chet Atkins, longtime record producer for RCA, who helped him get to the top of the charts, along with his manager Jack Johnson. He became the first black performer to appear at the Grand Ole Opry. He also appeared on "The Lawrence Welk Show," and his stardom was magnified as the first black male of country music. With many hits along the way, it was "Kiss An Angel Good Morning" in 1971 that became his million-dollar crossover single. He also gave Ronnie Milsap a hand up, allowing him to be Charley's opening act.

In his autobiography in 1994, Charley Pride detailed his battle with manic depression. I guess you never know the demons people suffer. Happy, smiling, and grateful to all of us for making his day special, Charley Pride was on his way to another town for another autograph session he was more than willing to do. Charley Pride reflects the old adage that the bigger the star, the nicer they are!

HOLIDAY SHOW
WOLS RADIO
FLORENCE, SC

Bill Pinckney and the Drifters

Bill Pinckney was a music phenomenon adored by beach music lovers and shaggers throughout the Carolinas, but was well known and respected the world over. He was the last surviving member of the original Drifters and was born in Dalzell, South Carolina. In his interview, he asked me if I had ever heard of Dalzell. I told him my husband was from Sumter, right next to Dalzell, and he said, "Well, maybe we are somehow related!" We had a ball chatting about his path to fame.

Bill grew up singing in church and even played baseball as a pitcher for the Negro Baseball League before going into the Army. He served during WWII and earned five bronze stars. After the war, he returned to music, performing the gospel tunes he loved in churches and that is where he met the other original Drifters.

"Money Honey" was their first big hit, followed by a remake of "White Christmas." It was amazing that he could sing many different parts, from tenor to bass to baritone. But Bill left the group before some of their biggest hits due to some disagreements with management. Not long after, Bill wanted to get back to singing again so he started "Bill Pinckney and The Original Drifters." The name certainly conflicted with the former Drifters, but Bill's new group thrived among beach music lovers.

Bill Pinckney won many awards in his lifetime and was recognized by President Clinton and Nelson Mandela for his achievements. He was entered into the Beach Music Hall of Fame in 1995 and Coastal Carolina University gave him an Honorary Doctorate of Fine Music in 2002.

While getting ready to perform in Daytona Beach during a Fourth of July celebration, Bill died from a heart attack at the Daytona Beach Hilton, but he will forever be remembered as a mover and shaker in beach music circles.

In February 2014, I went to the Alabama Theatre to hear the Drifters and was fortunate to meet Bill's wife. I told her I had interviewed Bill and would always remember his wonderful smile, hearty laugh, gorgeous head of white hair, and long white sideburns that could only be surpassed by his warm teddy bear hug. Then with tears in her eyes, she gave me a teddy bear hug and said, "Thank you for telling me that. You made my night!"

SOUTHERN STYLE
TIME WARNER CABLE
MYRTLE BEACH, SC

Jerry Clower

Popular country comedian Jerry Clower came to the South Carolina Tobacco Festival in Lake City, South Carolina, in 1981. He was full of sassy southern stories, a tactic he perfected as he traveled around selling seeds and fertilizer to boost his sales. Soon tapes were made and distributed and excerpts were heard on radios everywhere and before he knew it, Jerry Clower was a household name. By 1973, he had become a member of the Grand Ole Opry, appearing on television shows and in television commercials, even authoring four books.

Well, as a guest celebrity in Lake City, Jerry took the stage to a jam-packed full house of farmers and their families who had come to get a glimpse of this crazy man and hear some of his off-the-wall ditties first hand. He told stories about Aunt Pet and Uncle Versie, Raynel, Marcel, and the Ledbetter's. His famous "Coon Hunt" went platinum with more than one million in sales, and Jerry knew that's what the folks came to hear most. I still recall the last line, "Shoot amongst us cause one of us has got to have some relief!"

That day at the Lake City Tobacco Festival, I only got a quick interview with him due to the fact he was on a tight schedule to get to his next gig. But he was a hoot; as I interviewed him there among the crowd, folks continued to come up to him for his autograph, ignoring the cameras and me. Jerry kept signing and acknowledging his fans as he tried to keep his composure and answer my questions.

Jerry Clower, a bigger-than-life storyteller who delivered "Clower Power" wherever he went, died in 1998 following heart bypass surgery.

PEE DEE PEOPLE
WPDE-TV 15 FLORENCE, SC

Scott Davis & Tonia Kwiatkowski

Thanks to Fantasy Harbor's "Magic On Ice," I was able to interview several ice skating champions over the years, but rarely two at a time. Having been a fan of ice-skating ever since I was a kid, this was really cool for me. My grandmother and mother never missed a TV show about the sport, or a chance to watch the Olympics, Ice Capades or Disney on Ice.

Scott Davis was a national champion in 1993 and again in 1994. He continued to compete until 1998. He started experiencing vertigo issues and had to stop competing, but as he told me, he could not give up his passion. He was now doing ice shows throughout the country, including a version of "Grease" on ice. Scott talked about growing up in Montana, "a perfect place for lots of ice all year long." He said his goal was to get into coaching to give back what he had learned from so many of his mentors and coaches. I attended his show at "Magic On Ice" and he was marvelous on such a small rink, never skipping a beat.

Tonia Kwiatkowski was a silver medalist in the 1996 Olympics and three-time world team member. She retired young in 1998 and her goal was to teach and coach. She told me on TV that there was a difference, as a teacher shares knowledge, while a coach becomes a part of your every being.

Tonia was able to demonstrate what she was famous for while at "Magic on Ice," her jump into a triple lutz. While skating backwards she dug her skates into the ice and performed a move that no other skater had done before. She was also well known for continuing her education while competing and graduated from college with a degree in communications and psychology. She admitted not knowing what she would do with that later in life, but she was proud that despite all the long hours of mastering her sport she was able to achieve her educational goals.

I teased her about being called the "old lady" of figure skating as she was called, competing at 26 and 27 against skaters much younger like Michelle Kwan and Tara Lipinski. Tonia laughed and said, "I did it my way!"

SOUTHERN STYLE
TIME WARNER
MYRTLE BEACH, SC

119

Richard Petty

It was around midnight when someone rang the bell at WBTW TV 13 one Labor Day weekend while I was there doing cut-ins for the Jerry Lewis Telethon. We were on the air asking for donations fifteen minutes out of every hour, begging people to call in donations or better yet, come to the station and deliver the money in person. Usually after 11 p.m., no one came again until morning but this night was different.

The station doorbell rang at 12:15 a.m. I went to the door fearful to open it, as the police recommended we keep the doors locked after midnight. When I looked out, a gentleman in a short black zip-up jacket and baseball cap said he had a check for us. I said, "Stay right there and I'll get our director to open the door."

He looked nice enough, with a big smile and eager to give us money for the Muscular Dystrophy Telethon and I hated to turn him away. Just as I turned to go, the man yelled, "Tell him I'm Richard Petty!"

Well, I was familiar with the name from NASCAR, and knew that The Southern 500 was going on that same weekend, but I surely would not have recognized Richard Petty, not being a race fan. When I told Russell Smith, our director, that Richard Petty was at the door, he laughed and said, "No way! It's a kook. Don't let him in." Russell could not believe that I would not recognize Richard Petty and felt that someone was trying to pull one over on us. He suggested that I tell the guy to come back tomorrow, but something told me that this guy was genuine. It was strange, but I decided to open the door.

The nice man handed me a check for several hundred dollars and printed in the left hand corner, as well as in the signature area, was the name Richard Petty. He said he was busy all weekend, but wanted to do his part. I invited him to come into the studio and asked him if he wanted to appear with me on the air in the next cut-in, but he declined saying, "No, I did not come here for publicity." Nevertheless, I begged him to come meet our director, who I knew was a huge NASCAR fan. This was truly going to be the highlight of Russell's life!

When Russell laid eyes on the man as I was escorting him into the studio, he jumped up and said, "I'll be damned. I can't believe it." Richard hung around and talked to the after-hours crew for thirty minutes and agreed to be part of our cut-in at 1 a.m., which we also ran twice the next day.

On the air, Richard Petty told us about his incredibly crazy afternoon at the track, and his passion for making a difference in people's lives whenever he could, which is why he made an effort to get to the TV station. He talked about some of his friends in NASCAR and how the crowds fueled his fever for the sport. He also said he had watched us earlier that day from his hotel room, but this was his first chance to deliver a check to us.

It was very obvious Richard Petty did not do this for publicity. As a result, I became a Petty fan. What could have been a petty thief at the TV station door that night turned out to be none other than a sweet, genuine, and generous man, Richard Petty.

JERRY LEWIS MUSCULAR DYSTROPHY TELETHON
WBTW-TV 13
FLORENCE, SC

Maurice Williams & The Zodiacs

Doo-wop is associated with many groups of the '50s and '60s and Maurice Williams and The Zodiacs are among the most legendary. Most people don't know that Maurice is a proud South Carolinian from Lancaster, born in 1938. He loved singing as a child and was always trying to out-sing his sister. Like most singers of the time, he got started in church with gospel until rock 'n' roll came rolling along. Maurice and a few friends started a group called The Royal Charms, which later became The Gladiolas, and finally The Zodiacs, a name that came from a small model car.

There were many famous Zodiac songs but here is what I found out from Maurice Williams during my interview. The song "Lil Darlin'" was a hit on the R&B charts but never made it past No. 11. However, Canadian group The Diamonds recorded it and it went to No. 2 on Billboard's Hot 100. That fueled Maurice's fire for fame.

In 1960 their song "Stay" became a hit and is known as the shortest song to ever reach No. 1 on the charts. In 1963, the British group the Hollies covered the record and took it to No. 8. In later years, the Four Seasons and Jackson Browne reached top 20 with "Stay." Then in 1987, "Stay" by Maurice Williams and the Zodiacs was included on the movie soundtrack for "Dirty Dancing" and sold more records than ever. The song "Stay" certainly had staying power.

Maurice was such a sweet man and a gentleman through and through. He was also very laid back as he talked about the days of success and even now, he felt lucky to still be in demand. "If it wasn't for beach music, we might not have had the success we have had for so many years," he said.

Maurice told me that his song, "May I" was a big hit in 1966 but it was made even bigger in 1969 when Bill Deal and The

Rhondels had a top 40 hit. However, Maurice did not care, as he was still proud he gave birth to it! I loved that song and told Bill I had shagged to it many times at high school dances under the Zodiac label.

Again, one of my high school and college favorites making their way to my interview couch! Thrilling!

SOUTHERN STYLE
TIME WARNER CABLE
MYRTLE BEACH, SC

Ken Barry

Doug Williams and I never knew who was going to show up as we hosted "The Holiday Show." A day in the late '70s was typical, with guests talking about local community theater, a fundraiser for the Rotary Club, the Lions Club selling brooms, and the Florence Symphony's next concert. Then actor Ken Barry walked in accompanied by an entourage of folks from the Southern 500. Ken was known for his role as the widower farmer on "Mayberry RFD," a spin-off of "The Andy Griffith Show." Andy decided to retire from his show, and all the other characters kept going, playing their roles. "Mayberry RFD." ran for seventy-eight episodes from 1968-1971.

Ken was first a dancer, having taken tap since he was fifteen. He even taught dancing when he and a friend converted an old grocery store into a dance studio in Moline, Illinois, where he was born. Yet, he dreamed of much more. During his tenure at Fort Bragg in North Carolina, he won a local talent competition that enabled him to fly to New York to be on the Arlene Francis show, "Soldier Parade," where he won the entire national competition. His TV debut made him a star. He then returned to the Army one week later and became part of the Special Services Corps, entertaining troops all over the world.

Then he entered a different contest and got another shot at TV as he placed third in a talent contest for Ed Sullivan's "Toast of the Town" show. The performance led to an offer from Twentieth Century Fox and Universal Studios. They groomed him with more dance lessons, vocal coaching, and acting lessons. Ken went onto to do more acting than dancing roles, and became a big star for "The Arthur Godfrey Show," "Talent Scouts," "The Carol Burnett Show," "Mama's Family," and many more TV programs of the time. Ken also appeared in several Disney films.

When we met Ken he was the star of the Kinney Shoes TV commercial singing and dancing to their jingle, "The Great American Shoe Store." It was very obvious that Ken did not like being taken from one media to the other on this day. He never smiled, and seemed to be annoyed with our questions about "The Andy Griffith Show" that led to "Mayberry RFD." I recall feeling so deflated after a couple of minutes of interviewing him that I passed the microphone to Doug as if to say, "you can have the rest of Ken's lousy interview. I'm done." We were both shocked at Ken's less-than-friendly attitude. We deserved better and our listeners did, too.

Later we learned from the Southern 500 reps they were also taken back by his arrogant demeanor. They said Ken did not realize his contract called for him to make appearances with local media as a result of being a paid star for the Southern 500. This was not what we expected from anyone connected to "The Andy Griffith Show." Ken Barry was not very "Mayberry" at all!

THE HOLIDAY SHOW
WOLS RADIO
FLORENCE, SC

John Volstad and Tim Culbertson

In September 1987, Paul Vernon of Murrells Inlet hosted the Mickey Spillane Sportfishing Classic and Lite Beer Celebrity Tournament. Paul was the president of the Southeastern Sportfishing Association and together with Mickey Spillane threw the biggest fishing party in area history. Eleven Miller Lite All-Stars and many Hollywood and sports celebrities were there to try their hands at catching the big ones.

I was honored to be there as Mickey and I were recognized by the organization for our conservation efforts. My award was due to all the on-air work I did to promote good conservation, safe boating, eco-tourism, and ethical sport-fishing. Mickey's award was for his commitment to make Murrells Inlet the place that everyone wanted to fish, and for his goodwill in doing public service announcements about conservation.

Celebrities included major league pitcher Sparky Lee, outdoorsman Grits Gresham, Olympic gold medalist Bob Beamon, pro football players Ben Davidson and Conrad Dobler, surfing champion Corky Carroll, pro place-kicker Efren Herrera, American League umpire Jim Honochick, NBA All-Pro Sam Jones, skydiver Arch Deal, and others. Lee Meredith, known as "The Doll," did not arrive for the ceremonial kickoff but came later that night for the party.

Two of the Hollywood celebrities I got to interview that day were John Volstad and Tim Culbertson. John was very popular at the time as the "Other Brother Darryl" on the comedy show "Newhart" which ran from 1982-1990. He and his two brothers on the show ran a diner and did odd jobs always introducing themselves in this way: "I'm Larry. This is my brother Darryl, and this is my other brother Darryl." The funniest thing about John's part is that the two Darryls never spoke, until the last episode, when they yelled, "Quiet." In talking to John, he said it was the easiest thing he ever got paid good money to do!

Memorizing lines was left for all the other cast members. All he had to do was shrug!

Tim Culbertson was a handsome hunk. He was big into commercials in his early career and once served as "The Salem Man" for Salem cigarettes. He was also featured in Coors commercials, Secret Deodorant, and Schlitz Beer before getting into movies. He appeared in "Man Who Loved Women," "Live and Die in L.A.," "Cannery Row," "Cheech and Chong's Next Movie," and "Star Trek II." Tim's TV credits include "the Dinah Shore Show," "Love Boat," "WKRP In Cincinnati," "Battlestar Galactica," "Cheers," and "Hill Street Blues," just to name a few.

I also learned that he loved snakes and that many of his pets, as he called them, were in big-time movies. He claimed that some of the snakes had more credits than he did. Tim is also a well-known stuntman in the Hollywood scene, probably due to his incredible athleticism. He played football, baseball, basketball, and ran track in college. Tim was offered professional opportunities in various sports but chose acting instead. He said with a laugh that maybe after this tournament, he would become a pro-fisherman!

These guys were great fun and seemed to enjoy the tournament activities and parties as much as any of the other visiting celebrities. This was the largest group of stars and athletes to come to the area at one time, thanks to Mickey and Paul Vernon. Now all the other sporting events, especially golf tournaments, try to emulate it.

GRAND STRAND GAZETTE WBTW TV 13
MYRTLE BEACH, SC

John
Volstad   Tim
Culbertson

Senator Strom Thurmond

Most folks need no intro to Strom Thurmond, especially southern folks. Serving forty-eight years as a United States senator, he even ran for president in 1948 but was never without some controversy. First he was Democrat who later became a Republican. He fought the Civil Rights Act of 1957 with the longest filibuster of any single senator – 24 hours, 18 minutes nonstop. He married two Miss South Carolinas, and after his passing, it became known that he fathered a child at age 22 with his parents' sixteen-year-old African-American maid.

I first met Strom when I was a student at the University of South Carolina Regional Campus in Florence, which later became Francis Marion University. His accent was the most Southern I had ever heard and he dragged out every word as if he had marbles in his mouth. He flirted with me and all the other cheerleaders on campus as we were there in our uniforms to welcome him. As he hugged me, he ran his hand down my back and onto my butt. Some of the other cheerleaders attested to the same. I thought it may have been an accident, but it happened many times in later years. Strom was the king of "copping a feel," as the saying goes.

In 1973, Strom appeared on radio with his beautiful wife Nancy, who married Strom when he was 68 and she was 25. Their baby James was less than a year old and I held him as Doug, my co-host, and I interviewed Strom. He made many visits to our radio show over the years, and always walked around the restaurant of the Holiday Inn where we did the show live and shook everyone's hand. He was continuously politicking. Even if the dining guests were from out of town and did not know him, he stopped at their table to greet them with a handshake. Yet each and every time I greeted Strom at any occasion, I always felt like he was "feeling me up." During my tenure at WPDE,

Strom came for a TV interview and once again when he greeted me his hands made their way down my body. It was freaky. Yet this man was loved and admired for his dedication to the people of South Carolina.

Many years later in Myrtle Beach when we kicked off our Vivace! Arts Festival, Strom, who was in his late 80s at this time, came to our kick-off party. Again, he did that little squeeze and hug he was famous for, running his hand where a "Southern gentleman's" hand should never go. This time, instead of getting annoyed about it, I had to laugh to myself to think that Strom was still sneakily enjoying himself after all this time. And who knows? Maybe it was his devilish roaming hand that kept him alive so long. Strom lived to be 100 years old.

HOLIDAY SHOW
WOLS RADIO
FLORENCE, SC

PEE DEE PEPOLE
WPDE-TV 15
FLORENCE, SC

VIVACE ARTS FESTIVAL
PRESS PARTY

The San Diego Chicken

Folks are still arguing about which came first, the chicken or the egg, but Ted Giannoulas will tell you for sure it was the egg! Here is the story.

In the mid-'80s, Ted came to town and gave me the honor of interviewing him as The San Diego Chicken. He said in 1974 while he was in college at San Diego State, a rep from a local radio station came to the school and said he was looking for someone to hand out Easter eggs at the zoo. Ted said he and his friends all raised their hands. Then the rep said, "but you'll have to wear a costume." The rep then looked at Ted and said "Hey you, short guy. You'll fit in the suit best." In less than sixty seconds the wild and crazy antics of "The San Diego Chicken" was born.

The gig at the zoo was only for Easter Sunday, but Ted asked if he could borrow the costume to go to the opening night of the Padres game. The next thing you know, Ted began to do silly things: a soft shoe routine, harassing the visiting guests, hoodooing the other team. Before he knew it, he was making eight appearances a day, even making TV commercials as the famous chicken.

I asked him if he was the class clown and it surprised me when he said no. He said he always sat next to the class clown instead and learned from him as to what was funny and what was not. Ted admitted that he always wanted to be a comedy writer.

Sadly, Ted told me his father, a Greek immigrant, was mortified about the whole chicken thing. He wanted Ted to become something prestigious, certainly not a chicken. He refused to come to any of the games to see Ted in action, until three months before he passed away. But when he saw how everyone went crazy for Ted's chicken portrayal, he seemed to be so proud. Meanwhile, Ted's mother loved the whole thing, even making most of his costumes.

What started out as a gig for one day turned into forty-year career so far for Ted Giannoulas. May he have many, many more. It's a God-given gift to make people laugh and forget their troubles the way Ted does. I am thrilled I had the chance to meet and interview "The San Diego Chicken" who is still cackling in San Diego to this day.

GRAND STRAND GAZETTE
WBTW-TV 13
MYRTLE BEACH, SC

Gary Player

Stages Video Productions was hired to video several popular golfers and golf courses for AAA Golf Vacations in the mid-'90s. This was a project that was produced by Tom and Jackie Herron of Myrtle Beach.

I got to tag to along as my husband Chuck was scheduled to shoot a whole day with Gary Player at his home course in Florida. Gary was born in Johannesburg, South Africa, and is known as one of the greatest golfers of all time. I had heard a lot about him from Mel Sole of the Mel Sole School of Golf in Pawleys Island as Mel and Gary played the South African circuit together in the early days and he always said Gary was full of spunk and personality.

Our taping day with Gary was far from the perfect spring weather we were expecting; it was very cold but he handled it like a pro. All bundled up in a long, red-hooded sweatshirt, I spent the day toting Gary's jacket. Whenever he was demonstrating for the camera, he would say, "Little Red Riding Hood, do you mind holding my jacket?" That was my job all day, carrying Gary's stuff. He always referred to me as "Little Red Riding Hood."

Every time a guest on the course spotted him and wanted to shake his hand, he was eager and available. Gary was incredibly friendly and full of advice all day. For instance, Tom Herron was somewhat overweight and Gary, being the health nut and exercise buff that he was, told Tom to get it together and get some of that weight off before it was too late! He preached eating right and taking care of oneself as the No. 1 priority.

Gary also talked to us about the many golf courses he served as architect for, approximately 325. He said some golf pros say they are the official architects while others did the work, but he claims that he really is the architect of his courses. He also likes to talk about his "Stud Farm." I was intrigued by the title and teased him about it, but it is a thoroughbred racehorse farm established simply for breeding.

A lot of folks don't know that Gary has a foundation that supports a school in South Africa for 500 underprivileged kids. He holds charity tournaments all over the world to support the school, as well as nutrition services for those in need.

The AAA Golf Vacations project unfortunately was never completed because of a disagreement between the producers and AAA, but Chuck and I will never forget the day we spent with this warm and benevolent legend, Gary Player. What a terrific guy! As we were leaving he said to me, "Little Red Riding Hood, watch out for the big bad wolf!"

STAGES VIDEO PRODUCTIONS
AAA GOLF VACATIONS

Dr. Hook

No, this is not the predecessor of Dr. Phil, but rather the rock band. Their official name was Dr. Hook and The Medicine Show, shortened in 1975, and they were performing at a big gig in Florence so I got a shot at them.

Dr. Hook had eight years of continuous success in the '70s and I loved their songs "Sylvia's Mother," "The Cover of the Rolling Stone," "A Little Bit More," and "When You're In Love With A Beautiful Woman." What most people don't know is that the poet Shel Silverstein wrote the songs for Dr. Hook's first two albums, and then some others over the years as well.

Shel Silverstein is mostly known as a writer of children's books that have been translated into thirty languages and sold more than 20 million copies. "The Giving Tree" is one of his most famous books, but in addition he was a cartoonist whose pieces appeared in *Look*, *Sports Illustrated*, and *Playboy* where he received leading artist status.

Dennis Locorriere, lead singer, guitar, bass, and harmonica player, together with Rick Elswit, lead guitarist, were simply delightful as they told of screaming women greeting them in alleyways, and those who would throw themselves down at their feet in typical adoring fashion.

What fun being rock n' roll idols!

These guys were handsome and real charmers so it was perfectly understandable that women would adore them. They explained that Dr. Hook also found much success with remakes by other artists like Sam Cooke's "Only Sixteen." This was the early '80s and they enjoyed traveling around the country, and in their words, "helping fans relive the sensational '70s!"

PEE DEE PEOPLE
WPDE-TV 15
FLORENCE, SC

Harry Carson

I have never been much of a sports nut, but I am proud that I was a cheerleader in high school and college. I want to tell you about my friend Harry Carson who grew up to become a New York Giant!

Harry was well liked in high school. He played for Wilson High School, and then transferred to McClenaghan High School in Florence. I went to McClenaghan and we were elated to have such a talent transfer to our team. Harry was born to be a linebacker. He attended South Carolina State University from 1972 to 1975 and never missed playing in a game for those four years.

After college, the New York Giants drafted Harry and he spent his entire professional career, thirteen seasons, with the Giants. He served as captain for ten seasons. In 2002 he was named to the College Football Hall of Fame. In 2004 he was nominated for the Pro Football Hall of Fame but insisted they take his name off the ballot. He thought it was unfair that the media voted on this honor, not the coaches and players. However in 2006, he was nominated again and accepted, but in his speech he said nothing is more of an honor than having the support of your fellow players and coaches. It's not about the media.

Harry, who lives in New Jersey, is still active with the Giants organization and is a sports broadcaster who has been very outspoken on his 15 concussions from playing football. And in these later years, he blames his football career for his forgetfulness and mispronouncing of words, a post-traumatic stress type illness, asking the NFL to examine this serious issue.

But the Harry Carson I want you to know about is the one who has returned to Florence for many years during his career to raise money for the local Boys Club, an organization that benefited him in his youth. He loves to encourage young boys and girls to study hard and create a firm foundation to build on. He reminds kids, if he can do it, they can do it.

Harry appeared on WOLS Radio whenever he was back in the area, and we were all proud to have him and welcome this former Super Bowl champ back home!

HOLIDAY SHOW
WOLS RADIO
FLORENCE, SC

Jim Kelly

Sportscaster Jim Kelly is well known on the golf circuit. Most people don't know this, and I did not either until I got to do a series of interviews with him at the Dunes Club in Myrtle Beach, but Jim got into the business by playing hockey.

He attended the University of Toledo and not only did he play hockey, but he was Rookie of the Year in 1965. Then, he started calling the games for a local station, which led to other hockey announcing jobs on other stations. Jim was lucky enough to land a job with Golf Network Inc., which was heard on NBC Radio networks. This led to his next big job with CBS Radio. Along the way, he covered basketball, track and field, bowling, golf, and horse racing. Soon he became the sports anchor for CBS Morning News. After a stint in Boston, he was hired by ESPN from 1985-2002, during which time he earned an Ace Award for his coverage of the 1987 American's Cup.

After exiting ESPN, Jim moved onto CNBC, calling the Senior PGA Tour. As he said, he was always quick on the trigger in reporting the action and that's what shot him up the ladder of success.

While Jim was in town working on the PGA Senior Tour, he sat in on a couple of my show tapings at the beautiful Dunes Golf and Country Club. He could not believe that great view behind the club that peers out over the pool, swash, and Atlantic Ocean. He said he was mesmerized by it.

And he was right. Unless you have ever been back there, it's hard to describe this spectacular view.

Jim had fun asking questions of some of my guests, pretending to be my co-host, because as he said he only gets to interview sports folks and sometimes that gets old! But I assured him, it was bigger bucks than what I was getting!

But what Jim did not know is that a cousin of mine, who

worked for the Golf Channel, was staying at my home during the tournament. She said Jim kept flirting with her and inviting her to dinner. She was appalled because she was much younger, only twenty years old. Jim was older than her dad! One evening he even called my house to talk to her not realizing I was the woman he was going to work with the next day. However, I never let on to Jim I knew about his flirtatiousness with my cousin, but heard from other female media in town he was insanely flirtatious with them as well.

Hosting the PGA Senior Tour at the Dunes Club was a great bragging opportunity for Myrtle Beach. It was also a great opportunity for me to brag. For one moment in time, Jim Kelly was my co-host!

SOUTHERN STYLE
TIME WARNER CABLE
MYRTLE BEACH, SC

Patrick Swayze, Bruce Willis, & Will Smith

Press conferences have always been fun around town, whether Dolly Parton was coming to introduce a new concept for The Dixie Stampede and Pirates Voyage or Alabama was coming back to announce something new for the Alabama Theatre. However, there was nothing more fun than the press event for the opening of Planet Hollywood. This was first class all the way.

The media was invited to an evening celebration rather than the typical morning press conference, and we were asked to dress to the hilt as this was going to be a big shindig. Patrick Swayze, Bruce Willis, Will Smith, and several sports guys were going to be here.

Red carpets lined the pathway for all of us holding the golden ticket for entrance into the restaurant for the private party, while bleachers were set up outside for crowds to gather who would get to see the celebrities after the press party extravaganza. Big-beamed spotlights lit the night sky and live bands performed the hits of the decade.

Planet Hollywood was wild with all the memorabilia of the stars, but seeing Patrick Swayze there with his beautiful blonde wife, Lisa, was extra special. I welcomed them to town with a handshake and smile and he said they were thrilled to be part of this as it was their first trip to Myrtle Beach. Patrick was as good-looking up close as he was in the movies. Together, he and Lisa were like Barbie and Ken.

Food, beverages, and the meet and greet went well. Then the big bash outside began. Bruce Willis gave me a high five as he entered the main arena and said, "let's party!" He seemed like the only star that was totally smashed but he was certainly the one who seemed to be having the most fun.

Unfortunately, this was all being televised to use nationally the following week, and when the young girl reporter from the MTV network introduced the shaggers she stumbled all over herself. She called them "scaggers" and it went downhill from there. Plus the MTV host's interviews with the stars were simply awful. It was the only unprofessional happening of the night. They obviously sent a novice to emcee the televised portion of the grand opening, but probably I am the only one to remember that. Meeting Patrick Swayze, Bruce Willis, and Will Smith was so cool and I'm sure that's what all the other media recall most about that red-carpet night at Planet Hollywood.

PRESS PARTY
PLANET HOLLYWOOD
MYRTLE BEACH, SC

Clifford Curry

Clifford Curry was from Knoxville, Tennessee. He told me he loved all types of music and began singing in high school, earning money and getting lots of attention from girls! Over the years he had many bands and found his niche in R&B and beach music. He sang with The Echoes, The Five Pennies, Hollyhocks, the Bubba Suggs Band, The Fabulous Six, and The Contenders. As he said, "I like to get around and sing with lots of musicians who share my love of song." His most popular songs include "She Shot a Hole In My Soul," "Soul Ranger," I Don't Need You," and "I Can't Get a Hold of Myself." He has also penned songs for other singers.

Somehow, Clifford seemed quieter than his contemporaries who I interviewed in the beach music field. However, I saw him perform live when I was in college, and he comes alive on stage.

He said he loved coming to the beach because "People here get it!" He was referring to the love and passion that shaggers have for his type of music. "Without the shaggers and their love of R&B and beach music, most of the old legends would be dead to the world."

In 1985, Clifford was inducted into the Beach Music Hall of Fame along with Bill Pinckney and Maurice Williams. He released "Christmas Ain't No Time For The Blues" in 2011.

He is often seen performing in North Myrtle Beach shag clubs and riding in a fancy car at the SOS Shag Parade in North Myrtle Beach. Clifford Curry surely added a little spice to my TV show, as he does to all of his live performances.

SOUTHERN STYLE
TIME WARNER CABLE
MYRTLE BEACH, SC

142

Senator Fritz Hollings

I never liked interviewing politicians. It wasn't my thing. Especially in the early years of my career, I felt insufficiently prepared to tackle the hard-core issues. In my later years, I knew too much about these guys to remain sweet and innocent in my questioning, so I preferred to not interview them at all. Besides, I never liked to put someone on the spot. I never wanted to make a guest feel uneasy. I want to treat them the same way I would want to be treated if I was being interviewed.

Just like all the area and state politicians, Fritz visited "The Holiday Show" often. He was tall, handsome, and stern in his delivery but could break out in an infectious laugh in a moment flat. I loved to hear him say "Charleston." It was if there were four syllables to the word. That is where Fritz was born and he was proud of it, as well as being a Citadel graduate.

Fritz served as a Democratic senator from 1966 to 2005. He was the governor of South Carolina from 1959 to 1963, and his military career was equally impressive. Despite all this he was very down to earth. He fought for the poor and genuinely wanted a better life for all his constituents.

Just a few years ago, I ran into Fritz Hollings at an event in Myrtle Beach and I reminded him that I met him on "The Holiday Show" back in the '70s. He asked me what I was doing now, and when I told him a TV show in Myrtle Beach he quickly asked, " Well, how come you have not invited me to come be on your show?" I answered honestly that I hated interviewing political folks and kept politics as far away from the show as possible. Fritz said, "Politics makes the world go around. You can't escape it." He hugged me and departed.

Lucky for me, I did escape politics and politicians every chance I ever had. Give me features instead. It's what I prefer and love!

HOLIDAY SHOW
WOLS RADIO
FLORENCE, SC

Super Mario

I knew him as Claudio Montrosse, a chef at Villa Romana, one of the oldest Italian restaurants in Myrtle Beach. His brother Renaldo had been on TV with me cooking gnocchi and one of my favorite interviews of all times was with his mother "Mama Lucia," who came on my show to make homemade pasta. Mama could not speak much English, so she spoke Italian throughout the whole show while I spoke English. It was hilarious because I understood her and she understood me. I even did a TV commercial for the restaurant with her. Again, she said each line in Italian as I interpreted what she said. I loved Mama Lucia. Everybody did. She greeted all dinner guests of the restaurant with a big hug as if they were family.

Villa Romana's accordion player Michael Delgardo has also entertained on my shows over the years. He's like a stand-up musical comedian who can play that squeezebox like no one else I know. He is extremely talented.

Now let's get to Claudio. One night while I was dining at Villa Romana, he told me about his former life as a pro wrestler. At first I thought he was kidding because I had known these folks for many years and never heard this story. It was so unbelievable as Claudio was five-feet, one-inch tall and weighed 400 pounds.

He said he got into the wrestling ring professionally in 1993 and he loved it. The crowds were invigorating. The louder they were, the sillier he would act. He was called a brawler and known for his comedy and gimmicks. His alter ego was "Super Mario," hence his professional name. Having him on TV talking about this often-misunderstood sport was fascinating.

Today, Claudio has slimmed down for health reasons and does not even look like the same man.

He recently moved out of the area to be nearer to his

daughter but I'll always be thankful for the wrestling secrets and behind the scene theatrics he shared with me.

SOUTHERN STYLE
TIME WARNER CABLE
MYRTLE BEACH, SC

Ray Charles

The Myrtle Beach Convention Center opened to an enthusiastic crowd back in the '80s. It was going to help large groups come to the area, which means more economic development.

Mani Costa was a super guy who was hired to be the executive director of the facility. He had served in this capacity in other cities and planned a big shindig for the grand opening night, hiring Ray Charles to come to Myrtle Beach to wow the crowd with his piano skills and sultry voice. But no one knew why the press conference earlier that day was canceled until we got there that night for the main performance.

The new convention center was lovely and everyone who was invited was in awe of how beautiful it was. We all gathered in the lobby for a reception and then were escorted into one of the major halls for the concert.

Ray came out looking spiffy but seemed less than friendly. Actually, he said very little except that he was happy to be invited to come to Myrtle Beach. Then right in the middle of playing a song, he stopped and apologized to anyone who had paid for a ticket for this event, as the acoustics in this new facility were the worst he had ever heard. Had he known how bad it was, he said he would never have come. He said certainly a novice with no expertise must have been hired to handle sound.

People were aghast but Ray said he was going to continue his concert, just don't hold the bad acoustics and sound against him.

Later, we found out that Ray had realized how poor the sound was during rehearsal and canceled the press conference. Frankly, he almost canceled the entire show, according to Mani. Ray was absolutely right. Someone did goof on the acoustics and audio for the facility. I have emceed many events there and the sound is pitiful. There are always folks who come up to me and say, "We can't hear you. You sound muffled from where we are seated."

The grand opening of the Myrtle Beach Convention Center was a less than perfect evening for one of its biggest events and one of its biggest visiting stars.

GRAND OPENING
MYRTLE BEACH CONVENTION CENTER
MYRTLE BEACH, SC

Dennis Morgan

When actor, singer, and 1940s movie star Dennis Morgan showed up as a guest on "The Holiday Show" in the mid-'70s, I knew his name but not his face. He graced us with an interview on behalf of the American Cancer Society that usually brought a personality to town each year to raise money for cancer research.

The funniest thing to happen was that we asked the Holiday Inn to put "We're pleased to welcome Dennis Morgan" on their marquee by 10 a.m. knowing Dennis was coming our way. Needless to say, they did this the night before, and in the wee hours someone laddered up the neon sign and re-arranged the letters to read, "We welcome Penis Morgan." Well, none of us realized it until Dennis arrived with the local cancer officials and no one loved it more than him. He said it was a thrill for him to have his genitalia recognized in such a lovely way. We were mortified and referred to it on the radio as "someone murdered the marquee!" However, in all his graciousness, Dennis said he hoped whoever did it was listening because he wanted to thank them for bringing such prestige to an old-time movie star.

Dennis told stories of his leading ladies like Bette Davis, Ginger Rogers, Barbara Stanwyck, and others. Since his retirement from acting, he became a rancher and loved the farm life, as acting was not as much fun as it used to be. He had done a lot of "B" movies before getting his big break in the 1940 film "Kitty Foyle," which won an Oscar for Ginger Rogers. He said she was a delight.

In his very early days, Dennis was a radio announcer and went onto broadcast football for the Green Bay Packers. Born in Wisconsin, he loved to sing and in 1947 was named Singer of the Year by the Music Trades Association. He also considered a run for Congress as an avid supporter of Dwight Eisenhower but said it would have interfered with his family life. He adored his wife and three children and said he couldn't wait to tell his wife about his marvelous marquee welcome.

Dennis Morgan made many movies, including "My Wild Irish Rose," "Desert Song," "God Is My Co-Pilot," "Cheyenne," and "Christmas In Connecticut." He was passionate about the arts and arts education. He continued to support both up until his death at 85 years old in 1994.

HOLIDAY SHOW
WOLS RADIO
FLORENCE, SC

Dennis, me, Doug Williams

Jonathan Green

While producing a marketing video for the Franklin G. Burroughs-, Simeon B. Chapin Art Museum, I traveled with my husband Chuck to Daniel Island, South Carolina, to interview artist Jonathan Green. The art museum has a wonderful collection of his work and he has been very supportive the museum's efforts.

Jonathan's home was breathtakingly beautiful inside. The big, bold, primary colors of his paintings were a great contrast to the stark while walls. It was exquisite. Jonathan is known for portraying love and spirituality in all of his works. He told me that the women in his paintings represent those from childhood who made him who is his today, not only relatives, but also women of the church. His soft-spoken voice and gentle manner is so different from the boldness of his art. Gullah influences are evident in all of his pieces, as well as the culture of the Lowcountry.

As a child growing up in Gardens Corner, South Carolina, he always felt like an outsider. He was raised by his adoring grandmother and always felt resentful that his single mother was excommunicated from the church as a result of his birth. His homosexuality later made him feel more alienated and he clung to what made him feel best and accepted – his art. After attending the Art Institute of Chicago, he had a slow rise to fame. Little by little, the community got to know his work and started supporting its uniqueness. Jonathan recalled with me many of the city's movers and shakers who helped him along the way. One of them was his patron Richard Weedman, who is now his life partner.

Our interview went well and I offered to do some extra video while I was there so that Jonathan and Richard could use it in their promotion of Jonathan's art. We were flattered when these two lovely guys invited us to lunch at their favorite local hangout on Daniel Island. By the end of the day, we were scooting back to Myrtle Beach with a deeper appreciation of this internationally acclaimed artist. Jonathan Green is a true artistic genius.

STAGES VIDEO PRODUCTIONS
MYRTLE BEACH, SC

Governor Dick Riley

Richard Riley, better known as Dick, was born in Greenville, South Carolina, and attended Furman and USC. He served in the House of Representatives and the Senate before becoming governor from 1979 through 1987.

It's not often you get to interview the governor when you host a local talk show. The news people always have easier access as they usually go to Columbia for the story. But in 1978, Governor Riley came to Florence and appeared on "The Holiday Show." He was simply delightful, a very down-to-earth, straight-talking politician. Our show was fortunate to have been on the air for many years and was the only media outlet where you did not need an appointment. All the political party people brought their candidates to the show for an interview, especially the incumbents.

Then in 1983, Governor Riley came to Florence for a big Democratic Party function. I received a call from his press secretary that he would like to appear on my TV show. I have to admit it was not often I featured political folks, but no one turns the governor down! The boss was astounded that I got the governor on the show. Once again, Dick Riley was terrific on the air and off. He even posed for photos after the show. I love the one where he had his hand on my knee, something he did casually, meaning nothing by it. But there is a better part of the story.

In 1993, President Clinton made Dick Riley the Secretary of Education, a position he held until 2001. I was so proud of him and thought I'd write a congratulatory note to him in Washington. Along with the note, I sent the funny photo of him and I on the set of "Pee Dee People" with his hand on my knee. He sent a note back saying whatever I do, don't expose that photo to the media, it could get him fired! He said the media could make something look bad out of something totally innocent, which we all know is so true. He was being humorous, of course, and thanked me for my note and photograph!

THE HOLIDAY SHOW
WOLS RADIO
FLORENCE, SC

PEE DEE PEOPLE
WPDE-TV 15
FLORENCE, SC

Lash LaRue

I was never a fan of TV westerns, except for "Bonanza," as I had a teenage crush on all the Cartwright boys. So when Lash LaRue walked into the Holiday Inn and headed for our radio microphone I thought he was an Elvis impersonator. He had long black sideburns, slicked-back hair, and dreamy eyes. Doug, my radio partner in crime, recognized him right away and was excited to have the Cheyenne Kid joining us for an interview. He was the sidekick of singing cowboy Eddie Dean, who took down the bad guys with his long 18-foot bullwhip, hence the name "Lash."

Lash was in the area to appear at the Southern 500 in Darlington. He entertained us with stories of the B-westerns, his work with some familiar stars of the time, his love of the guitar, and his strong faith that led him to do quite a bit of evangelical work.

Lash found fame in the comics as his comic books sold more than 1 million copies around the world. He also starred in several episodes of "Judge Roy Bean" and in "The Life and Legend of Wyatt Earp," just to name a few of the early TV westerns. Then he made his living appearing at conventions, the rodeo circuit, and country music events.

Doug did most of the interview since I knew so little about Lash, but I did join in the conversation every now and then, and made Lash laugh when I called him an "ol' whipper snapper." And since he accidently appeared on the same radio show with political guru Tip O'Neil, it was hilarious listening to Tip ask questions to Lash! They were both infatuated with each other.

Lash, a Louisiana native, died of emphysema at St. Joseph's Hospital in Burbank, California, in 1996. Even though I was not a fan at the onset of the interview, I became one. This 1950s and 1960s TV cowboy, king of the bullwhip, knew how to lasso hearts and laughter.

THE HOLIDAY SHOW
WOLS RADIO
FLORENCE, SC

Storm

"American Gladiators" made its TV debut in 1989. It pitted athletes against each other as well against the show's own gladiators. Since I have never been athletically inclined, this was not my type of TV viewing. However, I became interested when a local woman told me her daughter Debbie was a gladiator on the show. She explained that Debbie was coming to town and she would love for me to have her as a guest on "Southern Style."

Debbie Clark, better known as "Storm," made $1,500 a day during her tenure as a gladiator. Her persona spoke with a French accent, which she said made her sound sexy. I asked her how she got such a great, muscular body. She replied that she had two older brothers who she had to contend with growing up, so she learned how to be strong and defend herself. She admitted to being a tomboy, but that she loves to sing. She said that is when she feels the most feminine. Debbie majored in psychology and loved working with kids but her love of working out led to bodybuilding and that led to being a trainer. All of this got her to auditions for "American Gladiator."

During my show, Debbie could not have been sweeter. Her mom was very active in the community and was thrilled I had her daughter on local TV despite the fact that she was becoming a national celebrity. Debbie's mom said that none of her friends watched "American Gladiator" but they all watched "Southern Style." She was so grateful I interviewed Debbie. I was flattered.

In 2011, I learned that Debbie was homeless and living on the streets in San Diego with her ten-year-old son. I was very distraught about this because I knew if Debbie's mom were alive, she would have taken them both into her home regardless of the situation. Both of her parents died within months of each other.

Debbie claims she left "American Gladiators" after a bad accident left her knee shattered. She married but soon left her husband over a domestic violence incident. She is said to admit to drug and alcohol issues but is determined to get her life back together for the sake of her son.

Sherri Shepherd of "The View" came to Debbie's rescue and offered to pay the rent and utilities for six months in order to help Debbie with a fresh start. Unfortunately, I never heard the outcome. Hopefully, "Storm" will get out of the rain and into the sunshine.

SOUTHERN STYLE
TIME WARNER
MYRTLE BEACH, SC

STORM is one of the "American Gladiators" on the hit athletic competition series produced and distributed by Samuel Goldwyn Television.

Joe Sinnott

In 1988 I received a call from my buddy Mickey Spillane that Marvel Comics would be having an event in Myrtle Beach and he wondered if I would like to interview someone from that organization. As you may recall, Mickey's Mike Hammer was made into a Marvel Comic strip.

I was never a reader of the comics but I knew I could wing it and have fun with this interview, and I surely did.

Joe Sinnott is one of America's greatest comic strip artists. In the business he is called an "inker" and is still in big demand. In 2007 his art appeared on two U.S. Postal Service Commemorative stamps and he continues today inking "The Amazing Spider-Man" Sunday comic strip.

During my TV interview with Joe, we talked about his love of drawing when he was a kid growing up in boarding school. He said he was lucky to have teachers who inspired and encouraged him to follow his passion rather than to side step it and take up another trade.

Joe's favorites when he was a kid were Batman, Congo Bill, and Terry and the Pirates, among others. He served in WWII, worked hard in his father's cement-manufacturing plant, and then got accepted into the Cartoonists and Illustrators School in New York City. He could afford it thanks to the GI Bill. He worked whenever or wherever he was needed and in every imaginable genre of the business.

Joe said he also use to do the art for Treasure Chest, a Catholic-oriented comic book that I remember reading as a child in parochial school. I was actually seeing Joe's art thirty years before meeting him. And in 1964, he penciled a biographical comic on the Beatles that I remember buying when I was as a screaming Beatle fanatic. Who knew?

Joe's more famous pieces include several "Captain America"

renditions, "Fantastic Four," "The Avengers," "The Defenders," and "Thor." He has won just about every award in his field and is very humble about each of them. I still have a beautiful letter of thanks from Joe with his "Spiderman" artwork that he sent after the interview.

He also asked for a copy of the entire show to prove to his kids and grandkids that he was really working on his trip to Myrtle Beach. He had the loveliest handwriting I have ever seen.

Thanks to Mickey Spillane, I met and interviewed an inker.

GRAND STRAND GAZETTE
WBTW-TV 13
MYRTLE BEACH, SC

Howard Keel

Having been a lover of Broadway music since I was a child, I was elated when Howard Keel came to town as a guest of the American Cancer Society in Florence appearing on "The Holiday Show".

He was born Harold Leek in Gillespie, Illinois, in 1919 and grew up in poverty. He told us that one of his teachers noticed that he never came to school with lunch, so she always brought him a sandwich. Later when he became famous, he showered her with tickets anytime she wanted them.

At twenty years old, Howard told us that he was discovered by his landlady who overheard him singing and encouraged him to take voice lessons. Howard hated his own voice. As a basso cantante he wanted to be more like his hero Lawrence Tibbett who was a baritone. "I would dream that I would wake up one day and be a baritone, but it never happened."

His agent suggested changing his name to "Howard" saying it was a better name than "Harold." They turned his last name around and reversed the letters because "Keel" really does sound better than "Leek."

He made his first public performance in 1941 in Handel's oratorio "Saul." In 1943, Howard married actress Rosemary Cooper. He briefly went on to understudy John Raitt in "Carousel" in 1945, but was soon cast in "Oklahoma!" doing something that has never been duplicated. He performed the leads in both Broadway shows on the same day.

In 1947, "Oklahoma!" commanded fourteen encores when it became the first American post-war musical to open in London with a full house and Queen Elizabeth II in attendance. Howard Keel was billed as the next great star. Fame, however, was not good for his marriage and his personal life fell apart. He then fell in love with a dancer from the cast of "Oklahoma!," Helen Anderson, but years later that marriage dissolved due to Howard's drinking. In 1970 he married Judy Magamoll, an airline stewardess who was twenty-five years his junior. They met on a blind date and fell in love shortly after. She did not know anything about Howard's fame since he was not performing at this time. When she learned about his past success, she was somewhat shocked.

Howard had a total of four children with three different wives.

Howard's other great credits included "Annie Get Your Gun," "Showboat," "Kiss Me Kate," "Seven Brides For Seven Brothers," "South Pacific," "Kismet," and "Paint Your Wagon," as well as many other Broadway and television shows.

In 1981, Howard's stardom rose again with appearances on "Love Boat," "Fantasy Island," and 234 episodes of his starring role on "Dallas" as the hot-tempered oil baron, Clayton Farlow.

The Howard Keel I met back in the '70s, was warm and wonderful, handsome and charming, and even humored me on the air by bellowing a few bars of "Oklahoma!" His voice was one of a kind. Combine that with his head full of thick gray hair and a bushy mustache that seemed to dance as he spoke, and you have one hot performer.

Howard Keel died in 2004.

HOLIDAY SHOW WOLS RADIO
FLORENCE, SC

Howard Keel on left

John McCook

One of the most gorgeous men I have ever met in my life was John McCook. From 1976 to 1980 he played Lance Prentiss on the daytime soap "The Young and The Restless." Since 1987, he starred as Eric Forrester on "The Bold and The Beautiful." In addition, John has appeared on dozens of prime-time shows.

In the late '70s, John came to Florence with a female soap star to help with the March of Dimes Telethon. I can't remember her name, but I will never forget his.

Other than being handsome, he was charming. All the women who came to the studio to meet him got hugs, kisses, and autographs. Hundreds of them came from all over the both North and South Carolina. The entire weekend demanded more security due to his visit.

I was not a soap watcher and was very candid with him about that, and I think he liked the fact that I did not throw myself at him like most of the other women did. But we really hit it off over the three-day event.

Several times during the weekend he would take me aside and told me how good I was at ad-libbing, interviewing folks, and that my stage presence was "masterful." Okay, I was flattered to say the least, but I wondered if he was just flirting with me. After the telethon he asked me if I was interested in moving to a bigger market. He went on to tell me Connie Chung's success story, who at that time was just making it big. He urged me to not waste my talent in Florence. I hugged him and thanked him for the encouragement. He gave me his address and said if he could ever help me make some connections, he would.

One month later, I dropped him a line and thanked him for his support at the telethon as well as his support of me. I mentioned that I was a homebody and probably could never move far from my family but was interested in pursuing commercials rather than news out of the market.

The following week I received a three-page letter from John repeating his support, reminding me that more women were needed in TV, re-telling Connie Chung's quick rise to success, and included a newspaper account of her move up the ladder. He said I was perfect for news and if all I wanted was TV commercials, I should get an agent who could get me the big bucks. But again, he said I was cheating myself because he thought I had the talent to make it in the big-time.

Okay, you too are probably thinking he was coming onto me, but the fact is he was married to the beautiful and leggy dancer Juliet Prowse. He was truly just being supportive. I responded to John's letter with much thanks, and said that if I ever get the guts to move to L.A. or New York, which were his suggestions, I would call him.

Well, you know the rest of the story. I'm still in this area and will be until I retire. Any regrets? None. As Frank Sinatra said, "I did it my way." I didn't get rich nor did I find fame but I made a wonderful career out of local TV and radio.

I never heard from John again, but I still have that letter in my antique music box with other tiny treasures from the past. Just knowing he believed in me meant so much.

One of the most fascinating things about WBTW in those early days of TV is that it carried both CBS and ABC programming since there was no other TV stations in the market. They had the dibs on all the soap operas and soap stars. When WPDE went on the air in 1980, WBTW became strictly CBS, while WPDE became the ABC affiliate.

MARCH OF DIMES TELETHON
WBTW-TV 13
FLORENCE, SC

Fabio, Jacopo, & Guy

Press conferences can be boring but not when you have two gorgeous Italian hunks on either side of you. I was asked to be the spokesperson for an event called "Taste." The show co-owner did not like to be in front of the camera so she hired me to handle the press event and to host the actual convention show several months later, even though that did not happen.

Fabio Viviani became a star on the Bravo network's "Top Chef," and even though he did not win, he was voted "Top Chef Fan Favorite." He was a go-getter, so to speak, because by the time he was 27 he owned seven restaurants, two nightclubs, and a farmhouse in Florence, Italy, where he was born.

Since his nationally televised cooking stint, Fabio has appeared on "Good Morning America," "Ellen," "Access Hollywood," and "QVC." His cookbook put him on the New York Times best-sellers list. He believes in farm fresh comfort food, go figure! Fabio's best friend and award-winning bartender is Jacopo Falleni. They are now business partners in California with Fabio's father-in law, living the American dream and loving it.

These two guys were full of themselves at the press conference and everyone loved them. Surely they were going to be the front-runners at the upcoming food extravaganza in May and women would flock just to get a glimpse of them.

They gave me a copy of their signed cookbook and said they looked forward to seeing me a couple of months later when the event kicked off. But that's where it gets sticky. Kara Saradamigni, who was heading up the show and had contracted with me, was not able to get the sponsors she had hoped and the monies were barely there to pull off the show. Plus, her cousin in New York was involved and the two did not see eye-to-eye on anything. Needless to say, I showed up to do the gig, and she sent word out to me in the convention center hall that she did not need me.

They did not have the money to pay the celebrities, much less me. I had been booked for six months and to get canceled the day of the event was so unfair and no way to conduct business. I was upset and shocked. Luckily, The Sun News food reporter was there to hear it all and wrote a story about the whole mess, including the upset vendors who did not get what they were promised, either.

I did go to magistrate's court and won getting an injunction against her for seven years, but never recovered a cent of what was due to me. You can't squeeze blood out of a turnip, as the judge said. There were several others in court who did not get paid by this woman as well.

Live and learn. Thank goodness, that was a first for me. But one very nice thing happened as I waited in the wings to start this gig that morning at the Convention Center. Guy Fieri, the Food Network star who was also making an appearance at the show, came over to me and asked me why I was so upset. When I told him how I was being screwed, he patted me on the back and said "Sometimes bad things happen to good people. Take my advice and always get your money up front like I do." Great guy, that Guy! I'm a big fan of his thanks to his kind gesture and really good advice. He took the time to care when he certainly did not have to.

"TASTE"
PRESS CONFERENCE

165

Mary Lou Metzger

As a kid I always watched "The Lawrence Welk Show." Next to the pope and Jack LaLaine, Lawrence was my grandmother's third favorite man. He even beat out my grandfather. I lived with my grandparents when I was a kid and one of the weekend highlights was sitting in front of the TV with a big bowl of coffee and chocolate ice cream in my lap watching the talented Welk cast. Among my favorites were the Lennon Sisters, Myron Floren on the accordion, Norma Zimmer, and Bobby Burgess and his many dance partners.

Mary Lou Metzger called me one day to appear on "Southern Style." She could not believe I knew who she was right away. She said usually she has to go through a long explanation about her long-standing gig on "The Lawrence Welk Show." She explained that her job now was promoting a traveling group of former performers in a Welk review-type show, and they were coming to Myrtle Beach.

Unfortunately, we were scheduled to be out of town for a wedding on the night the Welk crew came to town, so I did not get to see them. However Mary Lou's visit to the show was simply delightful. She truly did not look a day older than she did forty years ago. I could not get over it.

Bouncy and adorable, she told stories about the good ol' days and how they all really became "family" and found it hard to accept the fame that came along with it. She filled me in off camera with some of the good, bad, and ugly that took place among the cast. I was sad to hear that Guy and Ralna split up. They started out on the show as singles, became a duo, and later married.

"The Lawrence Welk Show" ran nationally for more than twenty-seven years. It can still be seen in syndication. What most people don't know is that it simply started out as a musical variety show in Los Angeles from 1951 to 1955 before it went national. Let's face it, it was happy, family-oriented, and made you feel like you had a night out on the town even though you never left the couch.

SOUTHERN STYLE
TIME WARNER CABLE
MYRTLE BEACH, SC

Jay Thompson

His name may not ring a bell with you, but Jay Thompson is a playwright and a very good one at that. Jay, together with others, penned the Broadway musical "Once Upon A Mattress," a comical adaptation of Hans Christian Andersen's fairy tale "The Princess and the Pea." It marked the Broadway debut of Carol Burnett and started her rise to stardom. This musical is being produced around the world today in community theaters, high schools, and colleges. Jay also wrote the book, music, and lyrics for the opera "The Bible Salesman," and wrote the song "Jimmy" which is sung by the lead in another Broadway musical, "Thoroughly Modern Millie."

Retiring to Myrtle Beach, Jay got very involved in the arts scene directing and producing plays that he wrote, as well as a few others like "Annie," "Sweet Charity," "Steel Magnolias," and "The Mikado," which all got great reviews. Jay himself would admit to having a warped but wonderful sense of humor but that's what made his following so popular. He packed the house with each and every show locally including his own plays, "The Oldest Trick In The Book," a one-act musical, and "Pocketful of Wry," a musical revue.

When Jay appeared on TV with me, he would bring his portable piano and whip out a tune. He would ask me to say one word, any word whatsoever, and he would create a song around it. I said "Aynor" and Jay went nuts with funny lyrics in a matter of seconds. That song was later featured in one of his musical revues.

My husband and I even went to New York to see "Once Upon A Mattress" in its revival starring Sarah Jessica Parker. Jay was there being wined and dined like Broadway royalty.

He told us that when the theater producers invited him up,

they offered to fly him there but Jay hated airplanes, so he took a train. It was fun seeing him in the New York limelight, but he was still the down-to-earth, silly, and sassy Jay I loved.

One time Jay was waiting in the studio to talk about one of his upcoming gigs along with musical maestro Brown Bradley, another very dear friend of mine. The guest on the air at the time was from the Clemson Extension and was showing various veggies of the season. When he cut into a very large cucumber, we heard Jay off-camera yell "ouch!" That cracked us all up: the guest, the crew, and me! Jay was just so off-the-wall with his humor.

He was also a big supporter of our first area aids organization. United Spirit For Aids raised funds for many patients who could not afford medicine, or the money they needed to return home to die in the arms of their families. Jay was relentless in the pursuit to help the gay community have a voice.

Then, we needed a favor from Jay as Stages Video Productions was asked to produce a complimentary TV commercial for Brookgreen Gardens. Usually Brookgreen spots were very upscale and artsy, not kid-friendly. However, after they created the zoological area with animals that were native to South Carolina, I suggested that we create a spot featuring children singing an original song about Brookgreen written by Jay.

He accepted the challenge and it was such a rewarding day as we shot this commercial with local kids who sang their hearts out. Jay was there too, and we teased him about directing the director of the spot, who was my husband Chuck. Best of all, we won an Addy Award for the best Public Service Commercial of the year for the entire region.

Jay Thompson's last eight years were spent in local retirement homes. He loved having friends visit who helped him recall the good times of yesteryear. Jay loved to laugh and reminisce about the foibles of theater, both professional as well as local.

The area has been incredibly blessed by the musical talents of Jay Thompson, which was most evident at Jay's memorial service June 30, 2014, when the community's theatrical elite turned out to celebrate his life.

SOUTHERN STYLE
TIME WARNER
MYRTLE BEACH, SC

BROOKGREEN GARDENS
TV COMMERCIAL
STAGES VIDEO PRODUCTIONS

Kenny Bernstein

Former NASCAR star and Indy Car team owner Kenny Bernstein made an appearance on "Southern Style" in the early '80s as part of a promotional event at the Darlington Raceway. He was full of adrenaline, on the air as well as on the track, and he was loaded with testosterone!

Kenny told me how proud he was being known as "The King of Speed," because he was the first driver to break 300 miles per hour in the first quarter mile. He was now driving funny cars and it was funny to hear him describe the difference of those versus other drag racing cars. His sponsor was Anheuser-Busch, which remained with him for thirty years, the sports' longest sponsorship in history.

Kenny was adorable, tanned, witty, and flirtatious. His time on the air was filled with great stories of his adventures in racing. He also talked about his racing favorites and even the tracks he liked best. He said Darlington was truly one of the best in the world. Then again, he was there representing Darlington, what else could he say?

After the show, Kenny hung around and interviewed me. He wanted to know how I got into TV, was it a full-time job, and could he take me to dinner that night? I assured him I had a boyfriend and he said he did not care. Then he became incredibly giddy and cute, begging me to accept the invitation. I told him I was a one-man woman. He laughed and said, "What a waste!"

As he left the studio, he abruptly turned around and yelled back at me, "If you change your mind, call me. You have my number." A few weeks later Kenny called and asked if I was still in the same relationship, and was so disappointed to learn that I was.

Three years later, I was thrilled he won his first funny car championship in 1985. Since then, Kenny married and has partnered with his son Brandon in the racing business until Brandon was critically injured in a race.

Kenny was entered into the Motorsports Hall of Fame in 2009 and retired from racing in 2011.

PEE DEE PEOPLE
WPDE-TV 15
FLORENCE, SC

"The Peter Adonis Traveling Fantasy Show"

So what's a nice girl like me doing with two male strippers from "The Peter Adonis Traveling Fantasy Show"? Yes, I asked myself the same question that morning as I drove to work.

You have to understand that in this business we have to appease many people, from the boss to all the salespeople who want to bonus their clients with a free appearance on the local talk show. Even when you are the producer and that means making decisions as to the content of the show, there is always the executive producer who can override you. That person is usually the general manager. There have been many times that I bucked a request to put a certain guest on the show because it was just too commercial, and I was applauded for it, but there were other times when the client was spending thousands with the station, that I had to figure out how to make the interview work. In this case, it was a no-brainer. The nightclub that hosted them spent a lot of money with the station, and I knew this would be fun and entertaining.

There was no question that "The Peter Adonis Traveling Fantasy Show" had great appeal. Everywhere they went they packed the house as well as their jockey shorts ... with money, that is! The two guys who arrived at the station were handsome but came to the studio looking like choirboys. I knew, of course, that they would not appear in skimpy clothing, but who knew these guys could look so sweet and innocent. They were nothing short of charming. It was amazing that they used to have REAL jobs before all of this. They told me that among their group there was a stockbroker, a real estate executive, an estate planner, and even a dentist. The main criteria to join the group is simply good looks and to be able to dance. One of my interviewees was even married. I asked him what his wife thought about it and he said when he comes home with his underwear full of ten dollar bills she asks me when is his next gig!

The guys admitted they could not do this forever but it was good, clean fun and good money for now. According to these handsome strippers, "We make women come alive again and there's nothing wrong with that!"

PEE DEE PEOPLE
WPDE-TV15
FLORENCE, SC

THE PETER ADONIS TRAVELING FANTASY SHOW

Mitch & Ewa Mataya Laurance

Many years ago, the area was lucky to land Mitch Laurance and his beautiful wife, Ewa, as local residents. They are both well-known celebrities who just wanted a slower pace of life. They bought a farm out in Conway with horses in exchange for the hustle and bustle of the big city.

My first meeting with Mitch was in a live television phone interview for the March of Dimes Bachelor Auction in the late '80s. He agreed to put together a date package that would be auctioned off to benefit the organization. I was the first executive director for the Horry-Georgetown Chapter of the March of Dimes, and one of the girls on the committee knew Mitch and conned him into doing this. He was most gracious to agree and helped us raise a lot of money.

Fast-forward a few years when I met up with Mitch again. He was now living in Conway, married, and working for Himmelsbach Communications, handling golf business. He felt that he was still close enough to Wilmington so that he could continue to pursue his acting career. Mitch is known for his work on "Santa Barbara," "Not Necessarily the News," and "The Hand That Rocks The Cradle." He and his twin brother Matthew were featured in margarine commercial back in the late '70s.

Here in the Myrtle Beach area, Mitch has remained involved in the golf scene, even hosting "On The Green" as seen on local cable channels, and orchestrating golf events to raise funds for area organizations. He appeared on TV with me for the "Know Your Score" golf event that raised awareness for prostate cancer, which Mitch was diagnosed with at a very young age. He urged men to get their PSA numbers and to learn their score because if caught early, prostate cancer can be cured. As much as he has done in the big leagues on television, Mitch still appears on local shows and does commercials to promote various products.

Mitch still travels around the country doing billiards

commentary for ESPN. And that leads me to his wife Ewa who I have only interviewed by way of the Sun Fun Parade. Mitch and Ewa received stars on the Celebrity Boardwalk one year, and as their convertible flashed down the boulevard, I interviewed them from up above at the Myrtle Beach Pavilion. They are both incredibly charming.

Ewa is known as "The Striking Viking." She is a gorgeous blonde from Sweden who has won many billiard titles, including the WPA World Nine-Ball Championship, and the International Trickshot Championship. She was the co-host of the game show "Ballbreakers," hosted "The Ultimate Pool Party" for ESPN, and continues with Mitch as a billiards commentator for ESPN. On top of all of this she has written several books and articles on billiards.

My husband Chuck and I have become good friends with Mitch and Ewa and have been thrilled to do some video work for them when the occasion arises. They are both are enjoying being grandparents. Mitch and Ewa are truly a dynamic duo.

SOUTHERN STYLE TIME WARNER CABLE
MYRTLE BEACH, SC

SUN FUN PARADE
MYRTLE BEACH, SC

Photo: Jack Thompson

Sherry Hursey

Celebrities came to Myrtle Beach annually for the Sun Fun Festival, but I don't think there was ever anyone who enjoyed it more than Sherry Hursey. She played Ilene Markham on "Home Improvement" and was as bubbly in person as she was on TV.

I interviewed her during the Sun Fun Parade and even had her on "Southern Style." She talked about her early days in Rutherfordton, North Carolina, where few kids wanted to grow up to be actors or actresses, but she surely did. Sherry has appeared on "Happy Days," "Dr. Quinn Medicine Woman," "NYPD Blue," "The Mary Tyler Moore Show," "The Rookies," "Matlock," and "Six Million Dollar Man," just to name a few.

Everyone in Hollywood fell in love with her accent, but many times she had to work hard to avoid "the Southern-ness," as she called it.

Sherry had so much fun in Myrtle Beach making so many friends, especially with Marilyn Chewning of the Myrtle Beach Chamber of Commerce who ran the Sun Fun Festival each year, that she returned many times over the years. She was giggly like a little kid about the area attractions and said if she could make a living here she would move here permanently.

As far as "Home Improvement," she said they really were like one big happy family, which we all know is not always the case with TV show casts. She said it was fun watching the kids grow up and how their characters developed throughout the years.

Sherry has also had several soap opera roles and continues her acting career today. It was always so endearing how she would sneak back into town to visit us all with great big hugs, as if we were her long-lost friends. She truly loved Myrtle Beach, and all of us associated with the Sun Fun Festival loved Sherry.

SOUTHERN STYLE
TIME WARNER CABLE
MYRTLE BEACH, SC

SUN FUN PARADE
MYRTLE BEACH, SC

Doc Antle & T.I.G.E.R.S.

Talk about monkey business! Doc Antle is a well-known animal owner and trainer who provides critters for national TV shows and movies. He has appeared on all the late-night talk shows and no one would believe that he makes his home in the Socastee area of Myrtle Beach. T.I.G.E.R.S., The Institute of Greatly Endangered and Rare Species, allows folks at a very high admission fee to tour the facility and see the animals up close and personal, including "Bubbles" the elephant. Plus, he has a retail location at Barefoot Landing where folks can pay to have pictures made with the baby tiger cubs.

Now Doc is not without controversy. There are some who say Doc himself is exploiting these animals by making money off them. Regardless, I invited him to come on TV and share his story. He brought a baby tiger and I was able to bottle-feed her. I felt so motherly, and was so into the baby that I hardly recall anything Doc said.

The next time I invited Doc, he sent Kira, a beautiful blonde who arrived with three chimps. As she let them out of their cages, the chimps were apprehensive at first, but by the time the cameras rolled they were out of control. One was eating the fake fichus tree behind the sofa, one was crawling all over me, and one had climbed up a little stepping ladder she had brought to the studio.

Before I knew it, there was an astronomical smell coming from the chimp on the ladder. Then I saw it, a pile of loose poop on our beautiful carpet on loan from our furniture sponsor.

This was the stinkiest mess we had ever had in the studio. I could barely finish the interview because all I wanted to do was gag. Then when the chimp started to play in the poop, I decided it was time to wrap it up five minutes earlier than I expected, but I did not care. This was disgusting and I did not want any poop on our sofa, or on me! I would just let the next guest fill the time, even though she was in the wings gagging as well.

No matter what we sprayed in the studio, the smell remained for weeks. As for the carpet, it was a goner! The furniture sponsor totally understood the messy malady and sent us over a new one. No more monkey business for me!

SOUTHERN STYLE
TIME WARNER CABLE
MYRTLE BEACH, SC

Ty Pennington &
"Extreme Makeover: Home Edition"

In 2007, the community came alive with the glow of national TV as "Extreme Makeover: Home Edition" came to town. It was miraculous how everyone rallied to be a part of this great event. It was to be super publicity for the area, but more importantly, Renee Wilson and her four grandchildren, who were living in the worst run-down mobile home, would soon have a beautiful new house to live in. When the children were asked what they wanted in their new place, they all said their own set of dresser drawers.

My husband Chuck and I were asked by George Durant, who was handling publicity for this project, to come out and video the entire behind the scenes. He knew that not everything was going to make the final cut for the TV episode and wanted to make sure that all the local suppliers were featured in some capacity and that the spirit of the event was captured for posterity. In addition to the final broadcast that would air nationally, we would also have our own "behind the scenes" video.

Hall Custom Homes and Classic Home Building and Design took the lead, and the community followed. The owners both appeared on TV with me recruiting volunteers. This was one of the best things to ever happen to the Myrtle Beach area as far as teamwork. Everyone gave their best for Renee and the kids. No egos were involved, just pure, unadulterated love and dedication for the community.

Renee and her grandchildren were ecstatic as everyone shouted "Move that bus!" so they could see their new home. It was thrilling to see, and a tremendous honor to donate our time and talents to something so worthwhile.

The TV stars were all lovely, and since the building site was open to the public they made an effort to mix and mingle with the crowds many times during the day. They all seemed like genuine folks, even the producers. They were not Hollywood types at all. Ty Pennington was head cheerleader and was very kind and generous to the local media, granting interviews even in the wee hours of the morning. He also spent time with the volunteers, thanking them for making this successful. Ty really came alive at the finale party at Revolutions at Broadway at the Beach. He loved dancing with all the women who surrounded him on the dance floor, including me. We were all exhausted from being up late hours over the past few days, but no one wanted to miss the party after all the hard work.

Even though it was a cold and rainy week, hearts were warm and filled with love. The spirit was contagious. I have never been a part of anything quite like this before. Thank you, George, for including us!

In 2010, the show returned to Loris to build a home in about 100 hours for the Suggs family. NASCAR star Jeff Gordon made an appearance. We were not asked to do a video for this one, but if we had we would have been there in a skinny minute.

SOUTHERN STYLE
TIME WARNER CABLE
MYRTLE BEACH, SC

EXTREME MAKEOVER DVD PROJECT
MYRTLE BEACH, SC

Cameron Adams

It's amazing how many young people in Myrtle Beach have gone onto big careers in the performing arts when there was not much in Myrtle Beach to give them the proper background.

Surely there are tons of dance schools and a couple of theater venues, but compared to most cities we are far behind. Let's hope that changes over the next few years.

Cameron Adams is an incredibly talented lady now performing in major Broadway shows. Her mother Sandra is a dance teacher and current choreographer for the Theatre of the Republic in Conway. It was Sandra's talent and that of her many dance teachers that fueled Cameron's passion to dance. While still in high school, Cameron was cast in "Big" on Broadway but it was canceled before she made it to the stage. But it wasn't long after that she got her big break as Zanita in the Broadway revival of "The Music Man" starring Craig Bierko and Rebecca Luker with Susan Stroman as the choreographer. Cameron was awesome. We rounded up a crowd to go up to New York City to see her. She took us back stage and introduced us to everyone.

Then Disney made a TV movie of "Music Man" with Matthew Broderick, and Cameron was cast once again as Zanita. Since then she has also appeared in "Oklahoma!," "Hairspray," "Crybaby," "Promises Promises," "How To Succeed in Business Without Even Trying," "Shrek," and "Nice Work If You Can Get It." Cameron has been cast in two movies as well. She has had a chance to dance and perform on some of the biggest stages, including the Tony Awards and Macy's Thanksgiving Day Parade.

When Cameron was on TV with me she praised Brown Bradley, music director for the First Presbyterian Church, who gave her voice lessons and her first taste of theatrics. I was honored to be on stage many times with Cameron during productions with the FPC Players under Brown's direction. Cameron was my little sister in "Annie Get Your Gun" and she was a force to be reckoned with even back then. She is what is referred to as a "triple threat": she can act, sing, and dance! What is the most impressive is that Cameron has charisma, onstage and off.

During my interview with Cameron she also praised Lou Layton, her theater instructor from the Academy of Arts Science and Technology school in Myrtle Beach, for helping her hone her acting skills. Still young, Cameron has a lot of years ahead of her. All of Myrtle Beach should be proud of this local girl who made it to the bright lights of Broadway. There are others up there in the Big Apple, but Cameron's success has outshined them all.

SOUTHERN STYLE
TIME WARNER CABLE
MRYTLE BEACH, SC

Chuck, Cameron Adams, Craig Bierko, and me,

Elizabeth Barron

"**I** had an affair with Congressman John Jenrette."

Guest psychic Elizabeth Baron, who drove from Myrtle Beach to Florence to be with me live on TV, made this shocking statement. First, let me say that I don't believe in psychics and have never booked one for any of my shows except when I was forced to do so by a general manager who was more concerned with ratings than in the well-being of the viewers. I do believe that some people possess a unique sensitivity or ESP-type ability, and when used properly can be beneficial in police investigations or personal betterment. Nevertheless, I believe that only God knows what the future holds, and anyone who tries to predict it is a fake. And that's exactly what I told the boss. However, when I repeated that belief to him, he almost tossed me out the window, and even more appalling, he attended the same church I did, so go figure. All he cared about was ratings, which is what usually matters most to station managers. But in television when your little local talk show is on the air opposite "The Love Connection" at the same time of day, you need to get "numbers" or ratings any way you can get them. That was what my boss believed!

Elizabeth was an internationally known psychic who lived in Myrtle Beach. She had helped police crack several cases throughout the country and was known for assisting with exorcisms. She had appeared many times on national television regarding crime and taught meditation classes to help others hone their skills. Her clientele loved her and believed every word that flowed from her lips. At the insistence of the station manager, I booked her for several television appearances but on her third visit she hung herself out to dry. She kept the live phone lines hot, answering one caller after the other.

"Will my boyfriend come back to me?" "Where is my wedding

ring?" "Should I tell my sister I had sex with her husband?" This was as close as I ever came to Jerry Springer trash TV and I was mortified to be a part of it. But thank goodness, not for long.

Just as I was going to the next caller, Elizabeth grabbed my hand and stopped me.

"Please don't take that phone call," she said. "I know it is someone who wants to slam me for having an affair with Congressmen John Jenrette, and yes I did, and yes I did get pregnant, and yes he is the father of my child."

I thought I was dreaming. I couldn't believe my ears. This can't be happening. Then she started to cry.

"Elizabeth, please stop, this is not the place to discuss such things," I said. "Let's go to a commercial break and we'll be right back."

Once I knew we were off the air, I said "Oh my God, Elizabeth what were you thinking?"

"But it's true," she said. "I just wanted to admit it before someone accused me of it."

"Well, please get down off the set because when we return after these four commercials, I'll be going back on the air by myself for the last eight minutes of the show."

She proceeded to leave the set, and my heart was beating a mile a minute. What on earth am I going to do on the air with eight minutes by myself? What am I going to say? Would the boss kill me for not continuing with the psychic hot-line garbage? I told the cameramen to tell the director I was staying with the phone lines, but I was changing the subject. And so I did.

"Three, two, one, cue."

"Friends, due to the guest's previous comments, I am continuing the rest of our show solo, but I need your help. Please help me fill the time remaining by calling in with some topics you would like to see me cover in the future. Remember, this is YOUR show. If you like our craft shows, let me know. If you like the medical advice, let me know."

Well, all the phone lines which were lit up with questions for

Elizabeth went dead, so I continued with another minute or so of gibberish, begging for calls, for what seemed like an eternity. Lucky for me the phones began to ring one by one with faithful viewers making requests for future shows and commenting on past productions. Their loyalty and support meant more to me that day than I could ever express. They saved me. And best of all, no one asked where Elizabeth Baron went.

However, while I was finishing the program, the general manager, who always watched the show from his office, had arrived in the studio and was scolding Ms. Baron for her blatant revelations, and assured her that she would never be invited back. Alleluia! I felt vindicated!

Meanwhile, he placed a call to the station attorney, who advised him to contact Congressman John Jenrette's office to describe what happened. Needless to say, the congressman's staff member asked us to make them a copy of the show and not air it that evening at 7:30 p.m., which was our usual procedure. Of course, we obliged. However, according to the station's attorney, it was not libelous since the congressman was a public figure. Not to mention he had made himself world-famous a few years before by admitting to having a sexual encounter with his second wife, Rita, on the Capitol steps in Washington, D.C. Besides, when reviewing the tape of the live show, the attorney commended me because I had done nothing to encourage her disclosures. In fact, I cut her off and went to a commercial break before she went any further. I was spot-on in how I handled the situation.

"Was it true?" everyone later asked me about Elizabeth's private life with the congressman. My response was the same line I gave the GM about psychics from the beginning: "Only God knows."

Elizabeth's career continued to thrive over the years with guest appearances on national TV and radio. She wrote a book in 1993 entitled "Prophets or Profits" in order to educate the public on fakes in the business, and in 2003 created one of the most popular websites on metaphysics. A documentary was produced on her life, "The Elizabeth Baron Story." On the website, the documentary is described like this: "A single mother awakens from a coma after being brutally assaulted in 1978, now realizing she possesses paranormal gifts that will change her life forever."

Elizabeth Baron died in January 2014.

PEE DEE PEOPLE
WPDE-TV 15
FLORENCE, SC

The Lettermen

One of my most recent thrills was assisting Scott Richards from EASY Radio in introducing The Lettermen at the Alabama Theatre. I loved this group ever since they made their musical debut. My mom had most of their albums, and later I started buying them as well. Their blend is second to none and sounds like one harmonious voice. Fifty years in the business, with a member change or two over the years, they have never skipped a beat.

As Scott and I entered the dining area backstage at the Alabama Theatre, we were told that lead singer Tony Butala would be out to see us in a minute to fill us in on some facts about the group for our introduction. Tony soon greeted us with a hug as if we were long-lost family. He seemed shorter than I remembered and looked so handsome in his striped bathrobe and slicked-back gray hair. He explained that as The Lettermen travel around, they often get introduced by local celebrities like ourselves who gather facts about them from Wikipedia, which he said is not always correct. So he prefers to fill them in on what is true. Tony was thrilled when Scott told him he was a movie buff and loved trivia. Tony told us how he started out as a kid in 1932 singing with the Robert Mitchell Boy Choir and appeared in more than 100 movies like "Going My Way" and "White Christmas" with Bing Crosby, and even had a part in the original movie "Peter Pan." He was so excited as he told us about his childhood fame. Yet nothing could compare to the fame he has had since starting The Lettermen back in the '50s when the threesome wore letter sweaters as a marketing ploy.

Our backstage meeting continued as Tony refused to go get dressed when the manager told him he had fifteen minutes to show time. He was genuinely having a blast telling us stories of yesteryear. He was incredibly proud that astronaut Neil Armstrong took their music to the moon and left it there with other contemporary goodies. Now The Lettermen brag that they are not only internationally acclaimed but also inter-galactically acclaimed, which is how I introduced them at the Alabama Theatre, in addition to their fifty years of experience in the business, seventy-five albums, and eighteen gold albums. Donahue Tea and Bobby Poynton, the other two Lettermen, also joined us backstage and could not have been lovelier. They both laughed when Tony started to brag about his Castlebrook winery in Napa Valley, as if to say, "here we go again."

The concert was outstanding. Their blend and harmony could only be out-done by their showmanship. The theater was 90 percent full of adoring seniors who knew the words to every song. And in addition to singing most of their top favorites, they each sang solos to add to the pizzazz of the night. Donahue got standing ovations for the two songs he sang about his kids, Landry and Lawson. He and his wife live in Tennessee and own a cattle ranch. Bobby, who was part of the threesome from 1988 to 1995, left the group to spend time with his wife and two children in Illinois, that he refers to as "fortune of the heart" but eagerly returned three years ago to "fame and fortune," still dividing time between work and family. His version of "Bring Him Home" from "Les Miserables" brought the house down. As for Tony, who is surely older than 80, his voice may not be as strong as it once was but he could still knock a song out of the ballpark! Top that off with two encores and the crowd got their money's worth!

One other neat fact we learned was that Tony started "The Vocal Group Hall of Fame" in his home town of Sharon, Pennsylvania, which has honored groups such as Alabama, The Eagles, Beach Boys, The Supremes, Simon and Garfunkel, Three Dog Night, Peter, Paul and Mary, and others. Yes, this is one of the best parts of my job, introducing and meeting wonderful entertainers like the wholesome, talented, and most charming Lettermen!

WEZV EASY RADIO   MYRTLE BEACH, SC

Arthur Kent

One of my favorite songs of the '60s was "The End of The World" sung by Skeeter Davis, so it was a big deal when I heard that the man who wrote that music was living in North Myrtle Beach.

Arthur Kent was gracious and came before my microphone many times to tell stories of Tin Pan Alley. As he spoke about those days gone by, I could almost feel the essence of the period as Arthur told tales about his glory days. He was a child prodigy who won piano competitions all over New York City starting at age 10. He played at parties, restaurants, and anywhere he was allowed to play. After getting his master's degree, he directed church choirs, offered piano lessons, even wrote a few musicals that were performed at various colleges.

After serving in the army during World War II, Arthur teamed up with buddies and wrote a song for Frank Sinatra, "So They Tell Me." His next collaboration for the Mills Brothers, "You Never Miss The Water Till The Well Runs Dry," received much acclaim, followed by "Don't Go To Strangers" recorded by Etta James in 1960. Arthur told me he was lucky to have met wonderful lyricists along the way, all struggling for their big break. When I asked him which came first, the music or lyrics, he said it varied. However, he said he loved the challenge of being presented lyrics one night and having the music ready in the morning.

Arthur's top-ten hit "Take Good Care of Her," followed by "I'm Coming Back To You" kept him in the forefront of the composing industry. He said he never expected to make it big in the country music field, but when lyricist Sylvia Dee wrote the beautiful words of "The End of the World" in 1962 as a tribute to her late father, Chet Atkins agreed to produce the record and chose Skeeter Davis to sing it. It zoomed up to No. 2 on the

Billboard Pop and Country charts and reached the top five on the R&B charts.

Arthur and Sylvia Dee continued their work together with "Bring Me Sunshine" for Willie Nelson, and "I Taught Her Everything She Knows" for Billy Walker. He told me he really got the "hang of it" and started to love the country genre, writing "Just Across The Mountain" for Eddy Arnold, "Little Acorns" for Hank Locklin, and "Wonder When MY Baby's Coming Home" for Barbara Mandrell.

One very funny story Arthur told me was that one day in the late '80s he got a huge royalty check and asked the music company where it came from. He was surprised to hear that the song "The End of the World" became a huge hit in Japan as a rock 'n' roll hit. He actually invited me to his house to hear it, and it was hilarious to hear the mix. But, as Arthur said, "I'll take it!"

Arthur Kent became a great supporter of the arts community in Myrtle Beach. He became the accompanist for many theatrical productions, working along with Brown Bradley and The First Presbyterian Players, and with Jay Thompson and his theatrical efforts. He assisted the Community Choral Society, now the Carolina Master Chorale, with their many performances and was very active with Ocean Drive Presbyterian Church in North Myrtle Beach where he and his beautiful wife Helen worshipped.

In 2009, the world lost a great composer. In 2009, the Myrtle Beach area lost a great friend.

GRAND STRAND GAZETTE
WBTW-TV 13

SOUTHERN STYLE
TIME WARNER CABLE

Dr. Laura Schlessinger

In the late '80s, Dr. Laura Schlessinger came to Myrtle Beach to speak to the local advertising club known at the time as CAMP, Coastal Advertising and Marketing Professionals.

This club was the local chapter of the American Advertising Federation. Dr. Laura, a marriage and family counselor, was quite the rage on national radio and TV as she dished out advice on a variety of subjects. She was known for her quick wit, sense of humor, and shock value.

Dr. Laura appeared live on TV with me early the same day she spoke to the club, and was very friendly and simply delightful as she discussed her miserable childhood that led to her success and determination to make a name for herself. She mentioned after the show she was going to speak to local advertising pros about sex in advertising and how we are so archaic compared to advertising in European countries. She told me that her appearances on "The Sally Jessy Raphael Show" gave her the fame she needed to finally have her own radio show, which was once the second highest in ratings after "The Rush Limbaugh Show." In later years she even had her own TV show and became a syndicated columnist.

However, her program at CAMP was something that all of us who were there will always remember. Dr. Laura first showed a video of some of the most sexually explicit ads that were currently running on TV in England, France, and Japan. Then she told us that Americans were very stiff and stuffy folks. She asked us to turn to the person on our left and say "vagina." Then she asked us to say the word "penis" to the person on our left. This was so embarrassing since there were many advertising executives there who had brought their clients with them to this luncheon to meet Dr. Laura. As for me, Matt Sedota, who at the time worked for WNMB Radio but is now at EASY Radio, was on my right and Jim Sellers with The Sellers Group and now director of Worship Ministries at Belin United Methodist Church was on my left. Thank goodness these guys were super cool even though they both blushed through the entire exercise. None of us could believe she was making us do this at what had always been a clean-cut business organization, and it still is. Dr. Laura's presentation was meant to loosen us up, and we were all shocked as the hour and half session got consistently worse. Even the club president who invited her was mortified.

Dr. Laura went on to have a very illustrious career, winning many awards for her efforts in broadcasting. She has written several books that offer advice on a variety of topics and became very controversial for derogatory remarks about gays and lesbians. Sadly, there have been many people who said that Dr. Laura had no business giving advice on family at all since she had several well-publicized affairs out of wedlock, posed nude for a former boyfriend who sold her photos to an Internet porn site, and admitted she did not mourn her parents' death since she said she had no emotional attachment to them.

SOUTHERN STYLE
TIME WARNER CABLE
MYRTLE BEACH, SC

Local Treasures

Saito

I've been fortunate enough to know several men who set my heart on fire over the years, but only one who set my pantyhose on fire! That's what you get when you invite a Japanese sushi chef to the TV studio with all the tricks of the trade, including a mega-Ginsu knife, sterno, and a hot hibachi.

With all the many restaurants in Myrtle Beach, there has never been a shortage of chefs to appear on cooking segments for my television shows. One day back in the mid-'80s (which sounds like a century ago) I placed a call to Nakato's, which at the time was the only Japanese restaurant in town, and told them I wanted to have a Japanese chef on TV to do some cooking. Well, I learned real fast to be more specific with my request. "Japanese" is exactly what I got, but this guy could not speak English!

Saito arrived at the studio accompanied by Gene, the restaurant manager, who said that Saito was going to cook, but would not talk on the air because he did not speak English. All Saito kept saying to me was, "I cook, but no talk." Great, I thought, fifteen minutes with him doing all the cooking, and me doing all the talking. This was going to be tough. But there was no time to regroup. We went live in fifteen minutes.

I began by telling the viewers that Saito was going to de-bone a chicken in less than one minute. Diligently, he rubbed his two knives together, flipped them in mid-air, and began his magic.

"Wow, really amazing! Well, at least for me, not for the chicken," I joked. I tried making conversation, bragging about his skills, but all Saito would do is nod. Then I told the viewers that he was going to prepare a chicken and vegetable dish for us, using the chicken he just slaughtered, but first he needed to chop up the oriental veggies. He sliced and diced like an artist preparing for an exhibit at the Louvre. Each piece was perfectly synchronized with the next one. Meanwhile, I narrated the moves like a play-by-play announcer at a sporting event. Everything was going great until he reached down to crank up the portable hibachi. Just as he did, a spark flew from the grill onto my leg and I watched in shock as my nylon stockings slithered into smithereens. I grabbed a towel Saito had hanging on his apron belt and swatted at my leg to stop the gaping hole from getting any bigger.

"Saito, my goodness, you set my pantyhose on fire!" And the man who could not speak English said clear as a bell, "Do we have to start over?"

"No, remember we are live. All the viewers just saw you set my pantyhose ablaze. Besides, I thought you didn't speak English."

Hysterically laughing, he said, "I don't."

"Okay, so I look like Second-Hand Rose from the waist down, but let's continue with the cooking demonstration."

Saito never did stop laughing. As he dribbled the peanut oil onto the surface of the hibachi, the grease splattered everywhere, like a rain shower from heaven, or should I say hell? There went another lovely silk shirt down the tubes, and with no clothing allowance this job got very costly at times. What a mess! Yet, as the interview continued, or should I say monologue, Saito held tight to his doctrine of not being able to speak English. I was left narrating the entire segment, trying to smile and keep my composure while the steam and grease made my eye makeup look worse than Tammy Faye Baker's.

Something good came out of it all, however. To this day, whenever I run into Saito at the sushi bar at Wahoo's Fish House in Murrells Inlet, he sends me free samples. He owes me, big time! His wife Sheryl says they look back on the tape of that show often and laugh their heads off.

This is just one of the many priceless gems from working in local television that could earn me a Daytime Emmy, if I could only get nominated!

SOUTHERN STYLE
COX CABLE
MYRTLE BEACH, SC

Dr. Elgie Nissan

It was St. Patrick's Day 1982 and I wanted to do something different on TV with an Irish twist. In an effort to feature guests from the throughout the coverage area, not just Florence where the station was located, I called a friend in Marion, Garland Sloan, and asked him if he knew a veterinarian with a good personality who would come on TV with an Irish setter and talk about the breed itself and answer the phone lines to give free advice. Garland said, "I know just the man."

When I called Dr. Elgie Nissan he asked me if this was joke. I told him, of course it wasn't. I really wanted to have him as a guest. He told me he would think about it and call me the next day. Garland also called him and poured on the encouragement, and got it announced in the Marion newspaper. So, with some hesitation, Elgie agreed to do it.

Dr. Nissan and the dog arrived looking spiffy. The dog even had a green scarf around his neck and all was going well as we opened the phone lines to live callers. One woman asked about flea collars and if they really worked. A man called in asking about heartworms. Another woman asked about the feline leukemia virus and how contagious it was to other cats. And then it happened. The next caller was somewhat reluctant as she said hello. However, I could tell by the way she asked the question she was serious about it. This was in no way an obscene caller. Those are usually delivered fast and then the caller hangs up. This woman delivered the question slow and deliberate and remained on the line.

"Doctor, could my ol' man get crabs from our dog?"

I looked over at Dr. Nissan who said, "She's kidding, isn't she?"

"No," I said. "This caller is serious and needs a straight answer."

While Elgie laughed his head off and the beads of sweat poured from his brow, I looked into the camera and said, "Ma'am, I don't think so, but let's ask the doctor."

Dr. Nissan responded, "No, he can't and if he tells you he did, divorce him!"

That surely was one of the funniest moments I ever had on TV in my entire career. I was used to obscene calls and we usually ignored them and went to the next caller, but I knew this was very different. Sadly, this caller needed an honest answer for a very difficult situation in her life. As for Dr. Nissan, he couldn't stop laughing, so I did not take any more phone calls but I continued to ask my own questions about pet issues.

After the show, Elgie Nissan said he was totally "freaked out" and was sure to be the talk of the town in Marion for the rest of his life. He told me to never call him again. He was done with live TV!

PEE DEE PEOPLE
WPDE-TV 15
MYRTLE BEACH, SC

Marge Stonebrook

Before it was even cool to be a female in politics, Marge Stonebrook became the first woman on Myrtle Beach City Council and the first mayor pro tem. She was so proud of it and should have been. She was a transplanted Yankee, as she described herself, and fought many causes that made a tremendous difference to Myrtle Beach.

Marge had a great personality, but when she believed something to be true there was no changing her mind. She was anxious to break into the "good ol' boy" club and she did exactly that. Marge would not let go if she saw that things were not right on City Council. She always stuck to her guns.

One of Marge's biggest fights was keeping dogs off the beach during the summer months. Up until now, it was a free-for-all with dogs and their owners parading up and down the water's edge, leaving their poop behind. Marge saw this as a health hazard to kids and babies who played in the surf. She was right. _Some on City Council did not want to rock the boat, but Marge was relentless in the fight.

She came on TV and when we opened the live phone lines, callers would bark just like a dog. Many must have gotten together to do this knowing Marge was coming on the show but she just laughed and said that her phone at home rings all hours of the night and the same thing happens. She said, "That's okay, I'm not doing this for me. I'm doing it to protect kids and others who wish to sit on the beach without a health hazard." She also said she walked out her front door the day before to find a bag of dog poop there for her. She just laughed about it.

It was a long battle, but in the end, Marge won. There were many who supported her and others who fought her tooth and nail. Dogs have their time on the beach in off-season, and during the busiest months, the beach is off limits to pets at certain hours.

Marge was one of the first people I grew to love in Myrtle Beach. In February 1985, one month before I started "Southern Style," Cox Cable asked me to co-host the Heart Telethon with one of their nightly news guys, Richard Green. I did not even know Richard before I said yes. Fortunately, he was easy to work with and a perfectly wonderful co-host to share the stage.

This event was live featuring local talent and politicians answering the phone lines and taking pledges. Hundreds came out for the great free show. Not everyone had Cox Cable in their homes, so the bleachers were always full of enthusiastic folks.

The telethon was the brainchild of Marge Stonebrook, who also started the local chapter of the American Heart Association. She convinced Kathy D'Antoni, general manager of Cox Cable, to give it a try. It lasted nine years. I became the telethon producer the following years, lining up all the talent, while Marge co-produced and lined up the speakers and phone operators. Richard and I hosted it every year together and respected each other's talents. It was a labor of love for a great cause.

As a newcomer to the community, I met everyone who was anyone while hosting the telethon. Some of the guests, like artist Harry Love, became lifetime friends.

As the Convention Center got busier, they were no longer able to donate the space, so the event fizzled out. Marge then turned her attention to building a senior center as a home for those older than fifty who wanted to play bridge, learn art, take trips and watch movies, and have a meeting and gathering place. She courted the Grand Strand Council On Aging, as well as the city of Myrtle Beach. Together with a hard-working committee, The Grand Strand Senior Center was built. Marge was also one of the founders of the Myrtle Beach Sister Cities program.

I could go on all day. I was truly a big fan of Marge's and spent much time over the years with her. I helped take care of her when she developed shingles all over her body. I would also fill up her bird feeder every day and water her flowers, because they both gave her such pleasure as she looked out her window during her illness. Marge's death from cancer left a huge void in the community. I still can't believe the city of Myrtle Beach has not named a park or building in her honor. She deserves so much better. Perhaps a dog sculpture somewhere near the beach would humor Marge the best! I can hear her laughing now!

HEART TELETHON
COX CABLE/TIME WARNER CABLE
MYRTLE BEACH, SC

SOUTHERN STYLE
TIME WARNER CABLE
MYRTLE BEACH, SC

Vanna and Marge

The Georgetown Lighthouse

It is really wonderful when you know you have made a big difference in helping something happen. All of us in radio and TV go about our business every day and hope to touch someone in a special way, or to enlighten the audience in some capacity.

In the mid-'80s, the Georgetown Lighthouse was scheduled to be demolished. It had been inactive for many years and was slowly deteriorating. Many people did not even know there was a Georgetown Lighthouse. There were news accounts of its future demise, and many people decided they wanted to save this historic structure so they started a "Save The Lighthouse" project. But preserving it was going to take lots of money.

Fundraising efforts began and John Henry, a well-known Myrtle Beach artist who was a very successful art director in Chicago before moving to the area, painted a beautiful watercolor of the lighthouse from a photograph that was given to him and prints were sold to benefit the preservation. They sold out in just a few weeks. Others were equally as generous with their time and talents as this was an important part of Georgetown's history that all agreed must be preserved.

One day I contacted Captain Sandy Vermont from Georgetown, an incredible storyteller and legendary character in the community, and asked him if he would take us in his boat to the lighthouse to do a story. We had become friends through many previous interviews. Sandy jumped right on it and agreed that he wanted to help save it. This was his chance to be a part of the preservation efforts.

My husband Chuck and I called John Henry and asked him to go with us on a day-trip in Georgetown, telling him we were going on a shelling excursion with Captain Sandy. We wanted to surprise him with this trip to see the lighthouse in person that he had painted. We spotted it twenty minutes after we headed up the Sampit River and into Winyah Bay. John Henry was tearful as he gazed at the lighthouse for the first time. I'll never forget the look on his face as he stood at the base of the lighthouse. It looked exactly like he had painted it.

With Chuck as the director, we got to work on our story. I delivered a plea to save this lighthouse. Standing there next to it I could feel its past and its hard work guiding boats to safe harbor in days gone by. It was very moving being there with John Henry and Captain Sandy who all felt as touched as I did that day. We were doing something meaningful and good.

No, I don't take credit for saving the lighthouse, but the televised feature surely helped. Our interview aired followed by tons of folks calling their legislators and councilmen. WBTW also ran our story on the 6 p.m. and 11 p.m. newscasts.

Friends, take a boat trip out to the lighthouse with Captain Sandy and see for yourselves.

Thanks to many passionate locals, the Georgetown Lighthouse still stands proudly, illuminating the past for future generations.

GRAND STRAND GAZETTE
WBTW-TV 13
MYRTLE BEACH, SC

The Waccatee Zoo

Chico the Wacko Chimp

You know what they say about kids and animals. My experience with animal antics far outweighs any craziness I ever had with kids and there was always plenty of fodder from the Waccatee Zoo. Let me start with my very first interview with the zoo owners.

Billy Roberts, local nurseryman, told me about his cousins in Socastee and how they planned to start a zoo. He gave me their number and I gave them a call and sure enough, they agreed to see me and talk about the future zoo. This was the first interview ever done by any media in town on what was to become the Waccatee Zoo.

Archie and Kathleen Futrell loved animals. He was a businessman who had several kiosks at the Myrtle Beach Pavilion and she was a schoolteacher at Socastee High. Over the years, they were able to take rescued animals onto their huge acreage, including many they adopted from circuses, and some animals that were in line to be euthanized. Kathleen loved birds and had a large collection of her own and Archie had a chimp named Chico who adored him, and vice versa. Plus they had snakes, goats, deer, and tons of peacocks that folks dropped off at their property, so the beginnings of a zoo had already started by accident. Even many school groups had been out to see the menagerie.

Let me fill you in on Chico. I am convinced if he were psychoanalyzed, he would be diagnosed with attention deficit disorder. He is truly the hyperactive star of the zoo, and he knows it. In his two-story condo-like cage he has every entertainment feature a chimpanzee could want, including a color television. His attire is "tourism" stylish, usually decked out in Hawaiian shirts and safari shorts, looking just like most of the visitors who come to see him. His favorite antic is opening a soda can and guzzling it down like there is no tomorrow.

During this TV interview I did with Archie on location for "Grand Strand Gazette," Chico was out of his cage on a leash and seated next to me on a haystack. He kept running his fingers through my hair so lovingly until he jerked my pierced hoop earring so hard I actually heard the cartilage rip. I came as close to cussing on the air as I ever have, but I kept my cool and kept talking, even though he tore a big hole in my earlobe. To this day, my earrings do not hang level.

It was as if Chico was jealous that Archie was talking to me. He couldn't stand it. I saw a jealous rage I had never even seen from another female!

Archie filled me in on the zoo and how he came up with the name "Waccatee." His farm was located on the Waccamaw River and the Socastee Creek, so he combined the names. He told me the zoo idea had been kicked around for years but he felt it was time to share it with the community and it would open in about a year.

The more Archie talked, the more anxious Chico got, but not half as anxious as I was. Chico was starting to pull my hair, which was funny at first, but then it got scary. Oh yes, he was on a leash, but it was getting more difficult to remain composed. I knew it was time to wrap it up.

I have another story that beats this one as far as Chico's wacko personality. On the zoo's tenth anniversary, I went back to tape a whole week's worth of shows for "Southern Style," and one of the cameramen stopped to talk to Chico before setting up the gear. While talking baby talk oh-so-sweetly to Chico, this five-foot chimp strew a handful of feces through the bars of the cage that landed all over the poor guy. I laughed so hard I had to go to the ladies room and re-do my mascara, but worse than that, the cameraman had to go to the men's room and completely hose down! And boy, did he smell lovely the rest of the day!

Just a few years ago, PETA tried to take Chico away from

the Futrells, saying this was not any way for a chimp to live. They complained about his cage. They complained about everything. But thanks to the many letters of support from the local zoo lovers and from former visitors to the zoo, PETA was unsuccessful in their custody battle. And knowing what I know about this darling's behavior, they should be thankful! All of us who know the situation know that this is the most loved and spoiled animal on the face of the earth. Even if the gates of the zoo were left open for hours, Chico would never leave this safe haven or Archie.

When Archie died, his obituary listed Chico and Jeff as his two sons. Today, Jeff fills his dad's shoes in the zoo-keeping business along with Kathleen, and has become Chico's new dad.

Most recently I was there taping "Inside Out" and Chico was imitating everything that Jeff did. If Jeff clapped, so did Chico. If Jeff ran and hid behind the big igloo house Chico lives in, then so did Chico.

Be assured that you have been warned. Visit the zoo and revel in the love and care the Futrells have for the entire clan, but get too close to Chico and you may revel in something you'd rather not revel in!

Clyde the Camel

It was a great day as we prepared to tape five thirty-minute "Southern Style" programs at the zoo. The weather was beautiful, not a cloud in the sky. There was no humidity, which is a big concern for TV crews as moisture sets up on the lens of the cameras, but it was terribly hot … 95 degrees! However, we were not the only ones hot that day as all the animals were in heat, and I'm not talking about the sweaty kind. This wasn't moaning and groaning, it was screaming and hollering like wild banshees!

Throughout every single taping you could hear roars of passion, squealing yelps of sexual desire, certainly not made for daytime TV, but we tried our best to ignore it even though we knew it would be heard by all of our viewers. After three tapings, and feeling rather horny from the whole experience ourselves, we decided to move the whole set over to the camel pen. We felt safer there, because Clyde the humpback camel, who had the most gorgeous eyes and eyelashes, no thanks to Maybelline, was living solo. No mate, no nonsense. Or so we thought.

Just as we were about to begin, I spotted a group of youngsters from the Friendship House Pre-School along with their teacher Mary Ellen Greene, and so I asked them if they wanted to be on TV. Shouts of joy and screams galore assured me that they did, so I gathered them around the camel and started the interview with Archie on how he came to own Clyde.

Mid-way through the feature, the cutest little girl with platted hair and colorful barrettes started pulling on my shirt. "Miss Diane, Miss Diane, look at that thing hanging under the camel." Hearing her every word, but trying to ignore her, and hoping that she could not be heard as we continued to tape, I attempted to ask a few more questions hoping what the little girl referred to, wasn't what I was thinking it might be! But she was relentless. Just as animated as she could be, she reached up and tugged on my shirt again and said, "Miss Diane, what's that?" as she pointed to his large manliness. Now, of course all the kids are looking at it too, oohing and ahhhing, when all of a sudden Clyde begins to urinate with the biggest deluge of water like a gushing fire hydrant. It was so loud. It hit the ground, tossing dust from the pen into the air.

"Look, Miss Diane, the camel's peeing."

Well, I could have stopped the tape but it was hot as blazes and I was anxious to get this done and get out of there. I knew we could edit it if we had to, but what happened next was so darn cute we would have cheated everyone if we made any changes.

The kids were all laughing, Archie was laughing, and Clyde appeared to be laughing, too. With that, I said, "I pee, you pee, the whole world pees! So what!" Okay, so it wasn't my most intellectual moment on the air, but the kids loved it and their high-pitched squeals and giggles seemed a great way to wrap up the interview. Clyde the camel was a hit, but the little girl stole the show. No, you can't lose with kids or animals on TV, and with both of them, you're sure to have yourself a winner.

Arnie the Armadillo

No one wants to catch an armadillo barehanded, no less one covered in feces! Yet, a girl has to do what a girl has to do! Tony Bolt from the Waccatee Zoo was scheduled for a TV appearance and promised to bring something very exciting with him that day. Well, low and behold, Tony comes plowing into the station saying that there has been an accident.

"What kind of an accident?" I asked.

"The armadillo pooped in his cage and he is covered in it!"

"Well yuck," I said. "Can you take him to the men's room and clean him up a bit? We only have fifteen minutes to show time."

"I tried," said Tony, "but he just kept trying to bite me. I guess the trip from the zoo into town was too much for him."

I can tell you the smell was horrendous. Prior to the taping we put a towel on our demo table and gingerly held the critter in place until the segment began, but just as I was introducing Tony, the Armadillo named Arnie started to hiss and give me the evil eye, and he was impossible to hold onto because he was so slimy from his travel mishap. Now I was slimy too and he slipped out of my grasp. Arnie took off like a bat out of hell and headed for one of the cameramen, who ran into master control to avoid death!

I yelled, "Keep rolling tape!" as I knew this was going to be one priceless interview and we needed to hang on for the wild ride! No one wanted to catch him because he was covered in the most awful smelling excrement, and because he was really angry, so the camera crew got shots of him darting from one end of the studio to the other while Tony tried to catch him by throwing the towel over his body.

I was laughing so hard, I was crying, still not knowing for sure whether we were going to start over or just run the show as is, but as you might guess, this was too good of a blooper to not share it with all the viewers. Certainly one of those moments that would have made "America's Funniest Videos" had we sent it in to them.

After Arnie was captured, Tony was so out of breath but couldn't believe I was NOT going to start over. He kept saying, "You're kidding me, aren't you?"

I said, "No, you just keep that smelly, squirming, armor-coated monster under a towel on the table, and tell us how an armadillo is supposed to behave and we'll finish this up."

Tony was speechless for the first time in his life.

This was surely one of the wildest and funniest tapings of my television career. The production crew and I refer to it as "The Day the Crazed Critter Conquered Time Warner Cable."

Herman the Horny Duck

The Waccatee Zoo sent Tony Bolt over with a frisky duck in hand for an Easter interview. As Tony told the viewers there are a lot of ducks around town, and tons of Canadian geese but this duck was very special because he was in the petting zoo area for the kids to see and play with when they come out to the zoo. He just loves people.

Tony explained why families should not buy little baby ducklings or baby bunnies or chicks for Easter as they grow up and wind up in a zoo, like Herman. Not to mention it breaks the kids hearts when you have to give them away.

I offered to hold him and he was very sweet indeed, looking up at me from my lap and quacking every couple of seconds. Fat, white, and fluffy, he seemed like a perfectly well behaved duck, until he jumped up on my shoulder, then onto my head. It was as if he trained to do this.

Tony laughed and I did too, saying, "Oh, he likes me, he really likes me," sounding a little like Sally Field at the Oscars.

Then Herman starting to bounce around up there, yes, on my head, and I thought he was dancing and even said, "How cute is this?" But when I looked up at the monitor in our TV studio, I realized Herman was actually humping my brains out as if I was another duck. I asked Tony what he was doing up there and Tony said he was in love with me and was doing what ducks do when they are in love.

"Yikes. Get this duck off my head!"

When Tony grabbed the duck he shot a wad of creamy substance in my hair, and before I knew it I took on a strong resemblance to Cameron Diaz in "Something About Mary." The camera crew was hysterically laughing. I wasn't however as I had three more half-hour tapings to go after this one, and my hair was going to look like crap. But keeping my usually good sense of humor, I said, "Well Tony, I thought Herman was just ducky until this. I hope he doesn't misbehave like this with the kids who come into the petting zoo area, but it does give new meaning to why you call it a PETTING ZOO. Heavy petting, that's for sure!"

GRAND STRAND GAZETTE
WBTW-TV 13, MYRTLE BEACH, SC

SOUTHERN STYLE   TIME WARNER
MYRTLE BEACH, SC

INSIDE OUT HTC
CONWAY, SC

Archie and Kathleen Futrell
Photo: Lou Williams

Billy Roberts

Billy Roberts is one of a kind. I met him one day while I was making a TV commercial at Chapin Department Store. I saw him and his wife looking at me as Chuck ran the microphone up my shirt. I wanted them to know we were married and wasn't letting just any Tom, Dick, or Harry run their hand up my torso, so I went over to them to explain. They giggled and said they did not think anything about it.

It was on this day that Billy told me his cousins were starting a zoo in Socastee. He was also very complimentary of my TV show "Southern Style," and told me Myrtle Beach was "brighter" since I had arrived. As you can imagine, we became instant friends.

Billy owns Roberts Nursery on 28th Avenue North, a business he inherited from his parents and one of the first of its kind for the region. Even though it has not been open for business for years, Billy still keeps the gates open for guests to come ask questions about landscaping. He has a real passion for helping people.

However, it wasn't landscaping that first brought Billy to my interview couch. It was ovarian cancer.

I got a phone call from Billy telling me his wife had died and he wanted to save other lives by telling women to ask for a certain test that could detect ovarian cancer even when pap tests could not. It is called CA-125. I had never heard of it, and as Billy said, most women had not. But he learned that if his wife had been offered the test, she might still be alive today. Needless to say, I booked Billy right away. He talked from the heart with tears in his eyes, urging women to ask their gynecologists for this test. He said don't take no for an answer and even if you have to pay for it out of your own pocket, it is worth it. You can bet Billy saved lives by telling women about this test.

Then I heard so many people around town talking about

Billy Roberts and his genius when it came to greenery, so I decided to book him quarterly to offer free advice on the show. He was awesome. If anything, he was too talkative at times! I'd ask him one question and he could go on for thirty minutes. I would tell Billy we only have twelve minutes for this topic, and that was tough for a man with so much knowledge. But folks loved seeing this Myrtle Beach native rip into topics galore on the show. Billy also did some history lessons on the show that featured some of his fabulous photography. He was the first person to ever tell me about the old racetrack in Myrtle Beach near the old mall site. And since Billy use to take pictures for the first newspaper in Myrtle Beach and provided many photos to other regional newspapers, he has a super collection of some of the oldest historical photographs of Myrtle Beach.

Over the years, Billy and I have developed quite a mutual admiration for each other. He helped me with the landscaping design for our new home when we built it. We talk often and have lunch together several times a year. I have never met a more God-fearing man with such integrity. He has the greatest love for this community. Billy says, "No matter what happens, find the GOOD in it." That's just one of the many life lessons I have learned from this dear man.

SOUTHERN STYLE
TIME WARNER CABLE
MYRTLE BEACH, SC

Dr. Harvey Brown

I have always believed TV should be a great tool to educate viewers, not just to entertain, so on all my TV shows over the years I loved to feature doctors and have them discuss their specialties and open the phone lines for questions. I was the first TV talk-show host to ever do this in Florence or Myrtle Beach, and I'm mighty proud of it.

Physicians have such busy schedules so getting them to take time for TV is always an issue.

Besides, in the early '80s, most docs saw it as advertising and frowned on it. When I was lucky enough to convince one to appear on TV, he or she always came from Florence where the studio was located. One day I decided to place a call to the hospital in Darlington. They told me about an OB-GYN, Dr. Harvey Brown, who was a real ham, had great bedside manner, and would probably love being on TV. Sure enough, he eagerly took me up on the offer when I called him.

Dr. Brown arrived at the studio thirty minutes before the live show as planned, but I was shocked to see that he wore a western shirt, boots, and a cowboy hat! As a matter of fact, when I went into the lobby to find him, I said, "Hi, I'm Diane and I was looking for Dr. Brown who is a guest on my show today," figuring this man was surely not the doctor. However, he threw out his hand for a handshake and said, "At your service!"

When I introduced him on the air I knew I could not ignore his non-traditional clothing.

"Meet Dr. Harvey Brown from Darlington who looks like he just rode in on his horse. He even dresses like this at his office and his patients love it!" Then I made a joke about him having stirrups in his office too but they had nothing to do with horses!

Dr. Brown was awesome. He answered all the viewer call-in questions with honesty and never flinched even though some of the questions were very personal.

Following the interview, I was called to the general manager's office. In a scolding fashion, he asked me if I was sure that guest was truly a gynecologist. I said he was sent by the Darlington Hospital. Days later, we received many phone calls and letters about having Dr. Brown back on the air. He was a hit! Needless to say, the boss begged me to get him back on as soon as possible; after all, it wasn't just about having a great guest, it was also about ratings, especially to the GM.

I was thrilled to have Dr. Brown on TV once a month for about a year. From his second visit on the show, I always introduced him as the "Galloping Gynecologist." He loved it and the viewers did, too. Best of all, he became a favorite guest of my skeptical boss.

PEE DEE PEOPLE
WPDE TV 15
FLORENCE, SC

Jimmy DeAngelo

He was known as "The Godfather of Golf" and the first pro of the Dunes Club. Just the mention of the name Jimmy DeAngelo causes people to react with a smirk and a giggle. Everyone who knew him has a story to tell because Jimmy spoke his mind. Don't ask him if you don't want to know, and if you don't want to know he will still tell you! He was a mover and shaker who helped to mold the world of golf in Myrtle Beach. He was loved and admired by many.

My first interview with Jimmy was a flirtatious one, to say the least. Being old enough to be my grandfather, even though Jimmy would hate me for saying that, he flirted with me and I flirted back. It was like the mating dance of the swans. Of course we had met at a cocktail party months before, but Jimmy was interested in promoting an upcoming golf tournament, and I was offering free airtime.

What fun we had together! In his gruff, northern drawl he talked about the early days of golf and how proud he was to be at the right place at the right time as Myrtle Beach developed into a golf mecca.

But it was his second interview with me that got Jimmy in trouble. Several years later, Jimmy wrote a cookbook that featured a little golf lore, a few Italian recipes, and some "shtick," as Jimmy liked to say. We spent one six-minute segment talking about food and the next segment about his real love – golf.

"So Jimmy," I asked him, "did you ever think Myrtle Beach would become the golf capital of the world?"

"I knew it had the potential, that's for sure."

And then came trouble with a capital "T." I asked him if he ever dreamed we would have a golf course in the area owned by the Japanese, referring to Wild Wing Golf Club. Jimmy responded, "You could have gone all day without bringing up the god-damned Japs. I'll never forget what they did to us at Pearl Harbor. And you can edit that out if you want, but that's just how I feel."

Then I replied "Jimmy, I can't edit them out, we're LIVE, remember?"

He said, "Oh, my God, my wife is going to kill me. And all of my friends who I told to watch are going to harass me for the rest of my life."

That evening when "Southern Style" re-ran, we bleeped out the curse word, but everyone unmistakably knew what Jimmy had said. He caught a lot of heck around town after that, and refused to come back, even though I was brave enough to ask him to do so. Lucky for me we remained good friends up until his death, and luckier for me he never stopped flirting!

SOUTHERN STYLE
TIME WARNER CABLE
MYRTLE BEACH, SC

First Anniversary

On my first anniversary of "Pee Dee People," I was totally taken aback by how my show was taken over by friends and family. That can happen easily when you are just the host and someone else is booking the guests, but I was also the producer and booked my own guests.

Each week I had to turn in a list of whom I had booked on the show to the station manager. In this case, he knew who I had scheduled to be there and he canceled them all, telling them I would get back to them the following week to be re-booked.

While I was in the dressing room getting dressed and adding layers of makeup, I spotted Doug Williams, my former co-host on "The Holiday Show," and wondered what he was doing there. He said he came to watch the show being done. I was thrilled because he was my mentor and best friend.

Just as I was getting my mic on to go live, Doug joined me on the set and said he had a surprise for me. It was a roast of sorts for my first anniversary. Doug took charge and told everyone there were special surprise guests behind the green room curtain. One at a time they would say something sweet about me and I had to guess who it was. Once I did, the guest would come out and join us on the couch. It was unbelievable that they pulled this off! My dad, my sister, my boyfriend at the time, a former teacher, and some friends all saluted me with lovely words. Then I heard my mom's voice. She said I was her Christmas angel ever since I was born, but when she came around from the curtain to face the camera, she was dressed like a duck. She even had a duck headpiece on. When I said, "Mom, why on earth are you dressed like that?" she just said "Quack, quack!"

My mom had nothing else to say. I later found out that she was scared to death about appearing on TV, but she figured if she did it in costume, it would be easier. That is just a small example of my mom's warped, but wonderful sense of humor.

It was a glorious half-hour being honored by those I love and having Doug there to host was the icing on the cake. After all, he was the one who got me into the broadcasting business and I'll forever be thankful.

PEE DEE PEOPLE
WPDE-TV 15
FLORENCE, SC

Lou Schuster

One of the greatest things about live television is the ability to take live phone calls from the viewers. I loved it! The instant connection is a real high. It gets your adrenaline flowing when you don't know what the caller is going to ask or say. My favorite topic for live calls was medical advice from prominent doctors. But we opened the phone lines for other "hot" topics as well. On this day, however, I received my worst live call-in ever! Prepare yourself, because in a million years you could never guess what was said.

The guest was Lou Schuster, the director of the Florence Humane Society. She worked hard and loved her job but caused quite a bit of controversy in Florence for being very judgmental about who was able to adopt an animal. She would not let someone adopt a dog if they did not have a fenced-in yard. If she thought you wanted to adopt an animal for the pure sake of selling off puppies, and not holding to your promise of spaying or neutering at the appropriate age, the adoption was off! And Lou met with quite a bit of controversy dealing with the city on shelter renovations. People either loved her or hated her.

We began our interview talking about the importance of spaying and neutering. She addressed her concerns for the overpopulation of stray animals becoming a health hazard to the community. Then we gently moved into the topic of enlarging the current facility, which was going to cause the city council to raise taxes, and you know how volatile people can get about that!

Well, there was no problem getting the lines to light up.

"How can I volunteer?" one caller asked.

"How long can an animal remain caged up at the shelter without going nuts?" asked another. And the third caller said, "Hi, Diane, this is Randy Propps. I have something to ask Lou

Schuster. ... What do know about sucking dog dicks, you bitch?"

Well, the black camera girl turned white, and the white cameraman turned red, and even though I was not in master control, I'm sure the director fell out of her chair! But keep in mind; there are no delay devices in small market television stations. They are much too costly for low-budget shows like the ones I have always hosted. So I was left to handle it the best way I could.

"Lou," I said, "I apologize for the indecent comments made by the caller."

"Are we still on the air," she whispered, which was always a question asked by a guest when anything went wrong.

"Yes, of course, we are live. But I want you to know that the caller could not have been Randy Propps, as he is a well-respected SLED agent in our community and would never use such language on the air. Let's go to our next caller."

"You're certainly not going to take another call, are you?" she said.

"Yes I am, after all, we have ten minutes left in the show and what could anyone say that would be worse than that?" Good answer, uh?

The rest of the show went off without a hitch, but Lou was pretty shook up afterwards. Can't say I blame her. So was I. But I apologized once again to her for the caller's crass remarks and thanked her immensely for such a good interview and for being such a good sport.

Now I had to face the general manager, but frankly I knew he was either in a meeting or out of the office because he watched the show regularly. I knew if he had heard the obscenities, he would have been in the studio at this point.

Upon seeing me, his first words were, "Did something happen?" And as I began to tell him who the guest was and what happened, stopping short of the infamous question, he said, "Did the caller use foul language?"

"Oh, yes sir. It was pretty bad."

"Did he use the F-word?"

"No," I said. "It was worse than the F-word!"

"What's worse than that?" he asked.

When I repeated what was said, he agreed it was worse! Then I told him about the caller using the name of a well-known SLED agent. That was all he needed to send out one of his popular memos to all the employees so that everyone knew what was said on the air, and how it was handled. Seeing that quote in writing hanging on the employee bulletin board was even freakier than hearing it on TV.

Finally, the GM picked up the phone and called Randy Propps, who was not the least bit upset. As a matter of fact, he couldn't stop laughing. He said in his business, he has lots of enemies; he just never had one of them be so creative in their retaliation!

My talk show was getting more and more popular, but unfortunately for all the wrong reasons!

PEE DEE PEOPLE
WPDE-TV 15
FLORENCE, SC

Merlin Bellamy

HERO. I can't tell you how many times I have heard this man referred to as a hero, more than anyone else I know. Merlin Bellamy was the police chief in the North Myrtle Beach area during the devastation of Hurricane Hazel in 1954. North Myrtle Beach was not incorporated yet,but the little communities on the beach's north end were forever changed after Hazel.

While Chuck and I were working on a documentary of Hazel, every single person we interviewed talked about Merlin and his team who went house to house to warn everyone that a hurricane was coming. There was no news media, weather channel or technology to get the word to them otherwise. He spent days at the police station after the storm before ever going home to his family. Merlin also helped to get the area cleaned up and protected homes from looting. Yes, just ask anyone in North Myrtle Beach who was there in 1954, and they will tell you about this incredible man.

Merlin Bellamy was like a big teddy bear. His arms could encompass you and make you feel like a million bucks. Having had him on TV many times, I loved to hear his rendition of Hurricane Hazel, especially after having interviewed about thirty people for the documentary. He never considered himself a hero, he was just doing his job.

However, while doing video work for the North Myrtle Beach Area Historical Museum, many folks interviewed told their stories of the Merlin Bellamy they knew and loved. His name came up more than any single person while producing the documentation for that project.

Once when I had Merlin on TV I learned that he hosted the first biker event for the Grand Strand. Love them or hate them, Merlin wanted to boost the economy in the area. He had heard of a group of bikers coming down from up north, and gave them a special invitation to come stay and play in North Myrtle Beach. Being a biker himself, he gave them a tour of the area and welcomed them royally. They returned year after year.

A few years ago after Merlin's retirement, the city of North Myrtle Beach honored Merlin with "Merlin Bellamy Appreciation Day." The place was packed. There wasn't a dry eye in the place when the proclamation was read to honor Merlin.

Not everyone I have had on TV and radio has become dear friends. There have been a special few. Merlin is one of them. I visited him and his wife Joyce many times in their Little River home, and they stopped by our office a couple of times to drop off one of Merlin's CDs. He loved to play bluegrass music in his garage with his friends and then record it for posterity.

When I learned Merlin was dying, I visited him weekly in the hospital, nursing home, and then at his own home three days before he died. That's where Merlin wanted to die; among all the things he loved and with those he loved most. His funeral was beautiful; Merlin's favorite hymns and bluegrass selections filled the air from up above. And that's exactly where Merlin was as well, up above with his Lord and Savior. North Myrtle Beach will never be loved by anyone more, or cared for better than it was by its greatest hero, Merlin Bellamy.

PEE DEE PEOPLE
WPDE-TV 15
FLORENCE, SC

GRAND STRAND GAZETTE
WBTW-TV 13
MYRTLE BEACH, SC

SOUTHERN STYLE
TIME WARNER CABLE
MYRTLE BEACH, SC

"Studebakers Live"

Long before dancing shows were popular with the networks, "Studebakers Live" was rocking and rolling as a staple in the Myrtle Beach area. Airing on Saturday and Sunday at 7 p.m., this show, originally produced by Cox Cable which became Time Warner Cable, drew hundreds of people to the popular nightclub Studebakers located at Kings Highway and 21st Avenue North to watch the show being taped. Thousands tuned in on the weekend to watch it.

Its first host bucked the director for more money and threatened to not show up one night for the taping if the director did not agree to cough up more dough, and guess who got the call to get her butt over to Studebakers that night in 1985 to begin hosting? I guess since I was already hosting and producing the daily talk show, they thought I was a natural fit. However, I am highly allergic to smoke and as much as I loved the music, Studebakers was not a regular hangout for me. Just like most clubs, it was laden with smoke. But I felt like I had to rescue the station and host the show at least until they could find someone else.

So all pumped up with allergy meds, I gave it my best and fell in love with the adrenaline rush of it all and hosted for seven years until the club owner no longer wanted to support it.

So how could the show be named "Studebakers Live" if it was taped, you may ask? We explained that on every show. It was taped live with no editing (on most nights) and filled with good clean fun (on most nights). We never knew who would show up to be on the show as we took the first five couples to sign up each night with the DJ, and gave them a chance to dance their hearts out to one song chosen by them. There were many DJs over the years but my favorite was Jim Morgan, who I now work with at EASY Radio. He loved the show as much as I did.

I picked the judges for the contest in advance and sometimes I even picked a visitor who just happened to be in the audience to join the judging panel. I was also responsible for the sponsors, the prizes, and all show content. I agree with the former host that the pay was lousy, but in those days, every little bit added to my bottom line.

As far as the dancing – it wasn't meant to be spectacular. It was folks just like you and me out there having a good time. Some nights we would have several shaggers, boppers, twisters, country dancing, and some who were just plain drunk, but it made for interesting television. The winners each week were invited back at the end of the year to compete in a dance-off for $1,000. Weekly winners came back for the finals.

Here's one of my best stories. Nat Adams was directing from his mobile van outside the back door of the club. By way of the three-camera shoot, he was able to see something that I was not able to see while this twosome was dancing. From where I stood behind the judges, I could not see that the female dancer was not wearing panties, but with each twirl, she unveiled all her personal stuff. On this night the crowds were louder than usual, but I had no idea why! As their dance came to an end and they took their bow, Nat came out of his van and into the club, asking me to come to the van. This normally did not happen as we usually taped straight through. When he asked me if I noticed her panty-less bottom, I said no. So he played the tape back for me. I couldn't believe it. No wonder the crowds loved it. We simply decided to continue taping and we would figure out how to blur the uncovered area for the actual on-air viewing. There is no doubt this couple knew what it was doing. They came prepared to wow the crowd. Thankfully, they did not win that night and we never had to see them again.

Another important part of the Studebakers story is the letter Cox Cable received from Neilson, the ratings people. They wanted to know what this cable company was doing on Sunday night at 7 p.m. that consistently beat the No. 1-rated CBS Sunday night show, "60 Minutes." Amazing, isn't it? We beat

"60 Minutes" for viewership in Horry County, and everyone in Horry County did not even get Cox Cable and Time Warner! "Studebakers Live" was quite the rage, and I loved hosting and producing every minute of it.

STUDEBAKERS LIVE
COX CABLE / TIME WARNER
MYRTLE BEACH, SC

Brookgreen's Gator

Brookgreen Gardens is one of my favorite attractions in all the Grand Strand. Even though it is America's largest outdoor sculpture garden, there is far more to Brookgreen than statuary, flowers, fauna, butterflies, deer, and otters. Here's something you don't hear about in their advertising!

"Southern Style" did not shoot out on location much since the production crew had many other duties that consumed them on a weekly basis. However, I once was able to talk the boss into letting us go to Brookgreen Gardens to tape a week's worth of shows.

We were all set with up in a lovely courtyard interviewing a guest when a storm came up. That is never a good thing when you have scheduled guests to come out at various times for taping. The director saw the sky turning darker and suggested we pause, go to our cars to stay dry, and regroup in thirty minutes at the welcome center.

I grabbed my purse and made a mad dash to get to the parking lot as the rain and winds picked up. As I was running along the edge of a lake in tall grasses, I thought I was stepping up on a log, when all of a sudden the log opened its mouth incredibly wide and started to gurgle loudly. I had stepped on the back of a six-foot alligator! Just as I did, a bolt of lightning shot from the sky with tumultuous thunder that may have scared me more than the alligator actually did. My scream frightened the crew who was running in another direction. They thought I had been struck by lightning! Needless to say, I was running twice as fast now that I had ticked off this gator. Luckily, he did not come after me, but he sure was not happy about me bouncing off his back. His hissing assured me of that.

When I got to my car, I was shaking like a leaf and had one heck of good story to tell the crew as I am telling you right now.

We continued our tapings inside, which was disappointing since we were at one of the most gorgeous gardens on earth. You just can't control Mother Nature. As for me, whenever I am at Brookgreen Gardens I never venture too close to the edge of the lovely grassy ponds because I know that alligator is still out to get me!

SOUTHERN STYLE
TIME WARNER CABLE
MYRTLE BEACH, SC

Ed Streeter

Ed Streeter of Conway Glass is a nice guy and, having interviewed him many times about various artsy activities in Conway, I thought it was a great idea when he asked to come on the show to talk about a glass-blowing class for the holidays. Ed and his wife Barbara are well-known artisans who attract many visitors to their shop to witness the waltz-like dance they appear to be doing as they blow glass vases, figurines, bowls, and such.

Ed arrived at the studio with gorgeous balls. I know how that sounds, but that's just it. If you let your mind wander, it will get the best of you and I am known for doing just that! But I kept a straight face (okay, maybe with a little smile or two) as Ed on the air discussed his new holiday promotion, "Blow your own Balls."

"How unique," I replied. "How long does it take?"

"Not long at all. We'll be doing it every Saturday in December."

The interview continued as Ed pulled a red ball out of his bag, and then a green one, and then he pulled a blue one out and said, "Lots of people want blue balls nowadays!"

"Yes, blue is a very popular color for balls," I said as I rolled this mottled blue ball in the palm of my hand. "And look this even has vein like streaks through it, how lovely!" Everything I said sounded so suggestive!

Brown Bradley and Howard Barnard of the first Presbyterian Church of Myrtle Beach, who were waiting in the wings as the next to be interviewed, completely lost control and burst out laughing. They couldn't contain themselves anymore with the blue ball discussion. That of course, made Ed and I snicker a bit so I changed the subject by asking Ed what other Christmas ideas he had for our viewers.

Changing the subject is always a great idea to help guests get on a better path, even though it may not make better television. As for Ed, he was delightful and I invited him back for a repeat interview the following Christmas as well. Yes, the topic was once again blowing your own balls and it was just as risqué the second time around.

Recently, I had Ed and Barbara on my new TV show, "Inside Out," and suggested we be very cautious as to not be too risqué. There was no way to avoid the name of the event, "Blow your own Balls," but we did avoid the blue ball conversation, thank goodness. But if you'll excuse the pun, don't blow this off your to-do list as it is really fun to do and you'll go home with balls you'll be proud of! See what I mean? There is no getting around the suggestive language!

SOUTHERN STYLE
TIME WARNER CABLE
MYRTLE BEACH, SC

INSIDE OUT
HTC
CONWAY, SC

Alligator Adventure

Fortunately, I am not afraid of snakes. Oh, I don't want to step on one in the yard or see one in my house, but I have no fear of holding them, thank goodness. I have had more snakes on all my shows than any other animal. I guess it's because folks rarely see them and are intrigued by them, so wildlife guests feel compelled to bring them along.

Every single TV show I have had over the years featured snake handlers. When I first started "Southern Style" there was an attraction called Snakes Alive that appeared with me. Then the Waccatee Zoo brought snakes, a local collector of reptiles brought snakes, but it was Alligator Adventure that brought in the biggest, frightening yellow boa constrictor. Yikes, I thought at the time. This could be dangerous, especially when the handler wrapped this boa around my body like you would a feather boa. It was so heavy I could barely stand. Plus, it's hard to think and talk when you are that scared! However, I did not skip a beat! Okay, maybe my heart skipped a beat or two, but no one noticed.

Alligator Adventure has been a tremendous attraction for the area and they always made for great show appearances. They brought in baby alligators, birds, and other fascinating critters. They have never let me down when I have called them, but then again they know that you just can't beat free publicity. One thing is for sure, no more boa constrictors!

SOUTHERN STYLE
TIME WARNER
MYRTLE BEACH, SC

Harry Love

Many of my radio and TV guests became my friends. Just ask them. I treated them all that way. But some became family. Harry Love was one of those. He appeared on my very first Heart Telethon as a watercolorist with the Waccamaw Arts and Crafts Guild. He was a charming gentleman who had only just moved to Myrtle Beach two years earlier, but had already made his mark on the arts community.

I invited Harry on "Southern Style" to share his renderings following the telethon and that gave me an idea to start an art segment each week, along with my weekly animal adoption segment and cooking segment. People loved it. The artists loved it most of all because they sold work right off the show. Harry helped me line up artsy folks throughout the community and got the Waccamaw Arts and Crafts Guild to take charge as to which artist appeared next.

Before I knew it, Chuck and I had volunteered to make free TV commercials for the Guild just because we loved Harry. Harry knew we were struggling in our first year of Stages Video Productions and refused our offer to do them free and paid us out of his own pocket.

Shortly after, Harry was entered in the national look-alike contest on the "Live with Kathy and Regis" as a close second for newsman Walter Cronkite. The area was excited when Harry made the top three and was flown to New York for the finals. While he was getting into his seat on the airplane, the stewardess moved Harry to first class. Harry believed it was because he spoke to the stewardess as he got on the plane, but when she said, "Mr. Cronkite, would you like a Bloody Mary?" he knew the special seat was not meant for him. He figured if he could fool the U.S. Airways staff, he might win in New York. And win he did. Harry became "The Walter Cronkite of Myrtle Beach" with national publicity to prove it.

Another title Harry accrued was one I gave him in a local press release that I prepared for the Carousel Horse Project, which we co-chaired to raise money for a future performing arts center. I called him "The Godfather of the Arts." He had nurtured the Waccamaw Arts and Crafts Guild, and helped to build the art museum along with Harry Charles, Bob Pickett, Harry Hartshorne, Carolyn Burroughs, Gaye Sanders Fisher, and others. He was the person who went to Rachel Broadhurst on Myrtle Beach City Council to discuss buying the old Rivoli Theater for a possible arts venue. Harry used to tease me about my kindness in calling him the "Godfather" rather than the "Grandfather of the Arts."

The Carousel Horse project was the largest art fundraising event in the area's history, raising more than $364,000, which was designated to help hire architect Steve Usry to draw up plans for the renovation of the Rivoli Theater near the old Pavilion site on Chester Street. Local artists painted the horses, and got paid $1,000 to do it. Horses were sponsored by businesses for $5,000 each, and then sold at a big public auction event at the Magic Attic at the Myrtle Beach Pavilion.

Even though Harry's dream has not yet become a reality, many others are still working on making it happen, including me. And while the old Rivoli was found to be too small for the needs of the arts community, the dream continues. Hopefully in the next few years, a performing arts center will become a shining star in the community right next to the Myrtle Beach Convention Center.

I was lucky enough to become Harry's best friend. He was also like a second father to me. I admired how he continued to fight for causes he loved from his bedside at Brightwater Retirement Center. Harry died the day after Christmas in 2013. I was honored to do the eulogy at his memorial. I reminded everyone that he had been a journalist, bomber-pilot instructor, corporate attorney, veteran, and artist. But the title he treasured most was "friend." He said you had to be one in order to have one. Harry had many: just ask around town. I miss him more than words can say.

SOUTHERN STYLE
TIME WARNER CABLE
MYRTLE BEACH, SC

Harry Love, Me, Liz Gilland
Photo: T-Bone Terry

Dr. Bill Bogache

Viewers always ask me if I have to do a lot of research for my shows, and the truth is no. First of all, I've always produced my own shows, which means lining up the guests, scheduling their taping time, and making sure the segment airs. This gives me the perfect opportunity to discuss the topic with them on the phone long before they arrive at the studio. Then right before the interview, whether live or taped, I personally sit down with each of the guests for that show and review the points to be covered, which helps them feel relaxed and secure most of the time. Besides, I always felt that if I knew too much about a subject, I might not ask the right questions that the unstudied viewer might have about the topic. In fact, while doing an interview about something I was very involved with in the community, I left out important questions, like where the event was taking place, because I knew all the answers! But there have been times when I had to head to the library to research topics. Remember, the Internet makes that easy now, but it was not around back then!

Grand Strand Regional Medical Center and Dr. Bill Bogache, a local urologist in Myrtle Beach, had scheduled a seminar on prostate cancer, so I called to see if Dr. Bogache would come on TV to discuss the disease long before it was fashionable to do so. Frankly, not only had I never heard it discussed on TV before, I was not even sure where the prostate was! Okay, so I knew it was part of the male's anatomy, but that was all I knew. So I got out my old high school biology books, lucky to still have them after all these years, and read up on the prostate.

Dr. Bogache was hesitant at first because many doctors felt appearing on TV may appear to be advertising. I assured him that being on TV could save lives and it was no different than the hospital advertising that he was speaking at the Senior Center.

With a little persuasion, he agreed.

First up on the show that next morning was artist Alex Powers, shy and reserved, but an internationally known watercolorist who just happened to live in Myrtle Beach. When I asked him to tell me about his award-winning piece of art that he brought to the studio, he said that he would rather not mention the title because it may be offensive to some. I said, "Well, it just won an international award, it can't be too bad!"

Alex replied, "I call it Pissing on the Icons."

I said, "That's not so bad," and the interview continued with him talking about his upcoming watercolor classes.

Up next was Dr. Bogache, who pulled a model of the prostate out of a bag he had carried into the studio. He said it would help show where the pea-sized cancer can form and how it can result in death if not treated early or removed.

We went live on the air, breaking new ground on a health topic for local TV. Dr. Bogache was handsome and charming but appeared nervous. In order to break the ice and make him relax, I said, "Wasn't Alex Powers' art lovely?"

Dr. Bogache replied, "Yes, but if he had used my term, voiding, instead of pissing, he would never have to worry about the title!"

Yes, laughter is good and that led the way.

Dr. Bogache began his passionate plea for men to have their prostate exams performed annually after the age of fifty, and said it was better to choose life than to worry about any of the possible side effects of the surgery. He also urged women to take charge of the situation and make appointments for the men in their lives, knowing that women are usually better at staying on top of these matters.

He then asked me to hold the prostate model, while he used a pointer to show where the cancer begins, but as I reached for the model, I had no idea that it had several sections, like a jigsaw puzzle and all of the pieces fell on the floor.

"I'm so sorry, Dr. Bogache, I've never dropped a man's prostate on the floor before!"

"Will we have to start over?"

"No, you forgot we are live. But if you'll just help me put Humpty Dumpty back together again, we'll get on with this interview." I snickered. He didn't. So I held the base of the model while he put all the pieces gingerly back into place.

The rest of the interview was testy at first. I'm sure Dr. Bogache was reliving the falling prostate incident in his head and was somewhat embarrassed, but then he started to relax. With grace and dignity, the interview continued, and we have become good friends through his repeat visits on the show. Plus, we attend the same church and Bill tells me still today, folks tease him how I dropped HIS prostate on the floor of the TV studio!

Thanks to all the physicians I have had on TV who gave of their time and talents to offer free life-saving advice, especially Dr. Bill Bogache, Dr. Sal Rini, and Dr. Bob Bibb who always answered my calls.

SOUTHERN STYLE
TIME WARNER CABLE
MYRTLE BEACH, SC

The Great American Water Show

The Great American Water Show was way before its time. Built off Highway 501, behind the old Waccamaw Pottery area, it was an attraction that would be a huge hit today.

With a ratings period coming up, which always seemed to put General Manager Jerry Condra in a tailspin, I was asked to find something in the Myrtle Beach area to help boost viewership in Horry County. I chose The Great American Water Show because it had just opened and I knew it was still very much a novelty that most people had not visited yet.

I was living in Florence at the time, so I called the owner Steve and asked if we could come tape a thirty-minute special there. He would have been a fool to say no; publicity is good, and this was not going to cost him a dime.

The crew and I, dressed in our summer best, arrived on a very hot day. We knew this was going to be a killer shoot because no one wants to tape in 100-degree weather midday. But the job had to get done.

The park blew us all away. There was a big lake built by the developers where a Cypress Gardens water skiing type show was going on. Actually, we were told that some of the talent came from Cypress Gardens in Florida. There were beautiful women in skimpy costumes skiing their hearts out. They were all incredible athletes. There were speedboats flying up ramps, sailing through the air, and splashing down just like a rocket. The best part was enjoying the water splashes that cooled us off.

The bleachers were half full of guests who enjoyed one show after the other. Following the ski show was a dolphin extravaganza. Bottlenose dolphins were flipping around just to be rewarded by pretty young girls who fed them fish. Then there was a rock 'n' roll type diving show with lots of antics that had all of them in the water by the end.

As good as this attraction was, it was way before its time in a location that was not considered in the heart of things. The show did not last, and I know the owners lost a bundle.

However, my thirty-minute special was a gigantic hit. It boosted ratings and was as slick as any special feature that had ever been done at WPDE.

PEE DEE PEOPLE
WPDE-TV 15
FLORENCE, SC

Rusty

People always ask me who my favorite interviews have been and I would say that most of my top ten are not celebrities, but rather people who opened their hearts to talk about their most private and intimate matters in order to help others.

I received a phone call one day in the late '80s from a man named Rusty. He said he would like to meet me somewhere privately to discuss a serious issue. I told him that I wanted to know more before I met him and that I would only meet him in a public place. He said he never thought about how intimidating this sounded, and apologized. After he told me what it was about, I agreed to meet him at Hot Stacks Pancake House and asked the manager to sit us in the back room for privacy.

Rusty was in his thirties, blonde, and handsome with a great personality, but Rusty had AIDS. He told me that he wanted to put a face on AIDS in our community. He was afraid to tell any of his friends or his employers in fear of losing his job. He said he wanted them to know that they could not catch this disease from him, and all he wanted was to be respected and understood. He asked me if he could "come out" on my TV show.

I told him that I would agree to it as long as it was done in the same way he was presenting it to me, not showy, but matter of fact: "I am gay. I have AIDS, but I want to continue to live a fulfilling life and make a difference for others in the future." And that was exactly what happened.

I confided in the TV crew so that they would not be blindsided by the interview. Rusty was nervous, visibly shaking, but moved forward with grace and poise in his delivery on air. He said that everyone at work was watching and he wanted them to know he would not put them in any danger. If he thought that his disease would harm them, he would quit. Rusty also explained how his parents turned on him when he admitted he was gay and he never returned home again. He was also joining other locals in the newly formed organization called "United Spirit For AIDS," started by a group of gay individuals. He felt that this group would help AIDS patients like him get the medications they needed to stay alive. I told him to sign me up. I'd be proud to join.

Many wonderful folks organized "United Spirit for Aids" but I always admired Rabbi Reuben Kesner of Temple Emanu-el for being the only member of the religious community to get on the bandwagon for this group. Others simply shied away from it.

Not long after the TV interview with Rusty, I was contacted by Rabbi Kesner and playwright Jay Thompson to be the host for a fundraising boat ride on the Barefoot Princess to raise money and awareness for AIDS patients. They said they needed a "token heterosexual couple" like my husband and I to head it up in order to sell tickets. We were thrilled to do so. The event was the first official AIDS fundraising effort in our area. We had a ball with entertainment, food, and seeing the sights as the boat drifted down the Intracoastal Waterway.

That night, all on board thanked us for helping the gay community in such a meaningful way. All I could say in response was that I had led benefits for heart disease, cancer, March Of Dimes, and the Grand Strand Humane Society, why not this?

Within a year, Rusty died. It was "United Spirit for AIDS" who paid for the funeral and sent Rusty's body back to his parents for burial. I wish they knew what a hero Rusty was by leading the fight against AIDS in our community.

A few years later, CARETEAM took the helm to help those with AIDS in our community.

SOUTHERN STYLE
TIME WARNER CABLE
MYRTLE BEACH, SC

Jack Thompson

Everyone knows Jack Thompson. His story is one that touches your heart. He and a friend hitchhiked to Myrtle Beach as teens looking for work and Jack got to understudy with a well-known area photographer. Jack loved it here so much he begged his parents to let him stay and finish school. Today, his passion for this community is endless.

The official historian of Myrtle Beach, as he is often called, Jack has documented so many sights, buildings, hotels, occasions, and the Sun Fun Festival since the '50s. His most famous photo is of the old Ocean Forest being imploded.

Jack is also credited for saving the Myrtle Beach Train Depot. He fought city hall and won! It is now a great meeting place, entertainment venue, and real pride for the city.

I interviewed Jack many times, some for documentaries we were shooting, but mostly for TV. He was always anxious to appear and share his photos with the TV audience, but he always seemed to forget the date we set up for his appearance. I always called every one of my guests the week before with a reminder of their live visit or taping time. But my good buddy Jack would still forget. Most producers might have said, forget about it! Find another guest. However, I knew Jack was a priceless treasure, and he was worth calling the day before and sometimes the morning of the interview. When you want to produce a good show, you sometimes just have to bite the bullet and go the extra mile. Jack was always worth the effort.

Jack also appeared on TV with me when he and his brother authored a book on Shoeless Joe Jackson. Being from Greenville, South Carolina, they both personally knew Shoeless Joe and defended his innocence in the "black-sox" baseball scandal. Jack also came before my microphone for his photo collage book, "Myrtle Beach Memories.

Having emceed so many events over the years, I am lucky Jack was my friend. He photographed me with Vanna White, Kelly Tilghman, and others. And having emceed the Sun Fun Parade for eighteen years, I am lucky to have had Jack there to photograph the activity and give me copies that I now treasure. Many of Jack's photos are here in this book.

Thanks Jack, for your friendship and for the love you have of this beautiful community. Both you and your photos are priceless.

SOUTHERN STYLE
TIME WARNER CABLE
MYRTLE BEACH, SC

GRAND STRAND GAZETTE
WBTW-TV 13
MYRTLE BEACH, SC

INSIDE OUT
HTC
MYRTLE BEACH, SC

Photo: Jack Thompson

Santa and the Dickens Christmas Show

Many years ago, the Dickens Christmas Show was making its debut in Myrtle Beach at the Myrtle Beach Convention Center and was managed by Myra Starnes with Leisure Time Unlimited. Myra called me in Florence, where I was working at WPDE-TV 15, to see if I would like to interview Santa and his real-life reindeer, antlers and all, on "Pee Dee People." Great idea! How can you lose with Santa Claus?

All donned out in his red suit and natural white hair and beard, Santa was a winner, but the reindeer was looking a little frazzled from the ninety-mile ride to the studio. On the air we talked about the Dickens Christmas Show, which would feature arts, crafts, decorations, a festival of trees, and all the hoopla of the holidays. All the booth vendors would be wearing costumes from the Dickens era, and kids could visit Santa's village and have their picture made on Santa's knee with a real live reindeer.

When out on the roof there arose such a clatter … not really, but it seemed to fit…

Just as Santa was describing his village filled with elves and snow, there was a loud burst of gas that sprung from out of nowhere. I knew what it was, Santa knew what it was, but did the viewers know? God forbid they would think that I did such a thing on the air, and I certainly didn't want them to think Santa did it, so I asked the camera to zoom in on the cute little marble-like pellets that had just landed on the floor from the reindeer's behind.

"Friends, please know that your TV is not experiencing technical difficulties. The noise you just heard was a legitimate one, but the gas you heard did not come from Santa Claus or me. That adorable little antlered deer has just relieved himself before God and everyone. I guess when you gotta go, you gotta go!"

"HO, HO, HO," said Santa. And everyone involved with the show cracked up laughing.

The camera crew went ballistic, Santa and I were hysterical, and the more we laughed the more the reindeer continued his antics. There were reindeer turds everywhere. Santa, trying to regroup his composure, said, "Well, Miss Diane, what do you want Santa to bring you for Christmas?" And all I could say was, "Santa, I'll need a broom, that's for sure." And we both lost it again.

Needless to say, Myra sat in shock and disbelief at the disaster that had just unfolded. She was mortified. But as I told her after the show was over, it was still good publicity, any way you look at it. I was never sure she was convinced. But one thing is sure, that was the closest I ever came to losing control on the air, and one of the best laughs I've ever had, albeit at Myra's expense.

The Dickens Christmas Show continued to make annual appearances with me on "Southern Style" once I moved to Myrtle Beach, but Myra always refused to bring live reindeer after that! Darn it.

PEE DEE PEOPLE
WPDE-TV 15
FLORENCE, SC

The Gift of Life

Back in the early '70s, I became very interested in organ donations. When I was working on "The Holiday Show" in Florence, a live radio format, I met many people who inspired me to want to do more to further the understanding of becoming an organ donor.

James "March of Dimes" Jones, a nickname he acquired from the many dollars he recruited for the charity, was well known throughout Florence as the legally blind black man who rode his bicycle all over town. His goal was to collect "as much as he could" in honor of his childhood sweetheart, who died from polio. He made regular visits to the morning show to talk about fundraising, something he had done for more than fifty years. What an inspiration he was that he never let his blindness deter him from doing something so worthwhile.

But as time passed by, James' eyesight became worse, and he finally became totally blind, which still did not stop him from collecting money. One day when he was on the air with us, I asked him about being blind and what it was like to never see his children or grandchildren.

James began to sing "Amazing Grace." Well, it was surely the most beautiful and tender rendition of it I have ever heard to this day. But I wondered what did this have to do with my question. As soon as James got to the line of the song, "I once was lost, but now I'm found. Was blind but now I see," I had my answer. After he finished sining, James explained that through God's Amazing Grace, he knew what those children and grandchildren looked like.

"Thanks to the love of God, I haven't missed anything."

James was one of the dearest people I've ever met. We became good friends, and I even sponsored his family to receive Thanksgiving dinner from the local Holiday Inn for several years until his death.

Call it ironic. Call it fate. But I call it God's intervention that on the same show that day was the local Lions Club, asking listeners to sign eye donor cards, so that long after they are gone, their eyes will help someone else to see. I was touched. I was moved. I was determined to make a difference. Immediately, I signed the eye donor card right there on the radio show. Then I offered to go to civic club luncheons to help the Lions Club with their mission. I put together a fifteen-minute presentation that I took on the road, and as people left the luncheon to go back to work, I handed them a card to sign that they would put in their wallets alerting everyone they were an eye-donor. Okay, I admit it was a hard sell. Some signed the cards on the spot. Most took them home, probably tossing them in the trashcan.

Then, I figured if I'm going to spend time recruiting corneas, why not recruit all organ donations? I contacted the Medical University of South Carolina in Charleston, which was the only organization in the state handling such things at that time. They advised me to call the South Carolina Kidney Association, whose need for kidney donations spurred them into promoting all organ donations.

Before I knew it, I was going to Rotary, Sertoma, Civitan, and Lions clubs to ask people to discuss their desire to donate their organs with their loved ones, and to get their donor cards into their wallets. That continued for about three years. Organ procurement remains a passion of mine still today, and it all began with James Jones.

While I was hosting "Pee Dee People" on WPDE, a young Florence businesswoman and mother, Ann Daniels, was waiting for a heart. All of Florence was buzzing with fundraisers to help her raise the money she needed for the surgery should an organ be found. This was the first heart transplant in the state so it was big news. Ann appeared on TV with me before and after the surgery, but sadly lost her battle when her body rejected the new organ. I was proud to have emceed several fundraisers for Ann. She was very brave with her story and grateful to all of Florence for their support.

After moving to Myrtle Beach, my best resource to reaching people to become donors has been through television. Fortunately, there is now the South Carolina Organ Procurement Agency or SCOPA, as it is often called, and they have set up several incredible interviews with me that have certainly bolstered the donor program.

Mary Hill of Loris shared an incredible story with me on TV. Her daughter Kendra was in the emergency room with head trauma from a horrible automobile accident. While she was waiting to hear if her daughter would survive, another mother arrived whose son was near death due to liver failure. While Kendra was put on life support with no hope of recovering, the doctors talked to Mary about organ donation, a topic she never thought about before. Mary knew that Kendra's organs could help others and agreed to donate whatever could be salvaged from Kendra's body. Mary mentioned to the nurses that she knew there was another mother in the waiting room praying for her son to get a liver, but the nurses said a lot of testing must be done to see if he and Kendra could possibly be match. There was a lot of protocol that they must follow.

Mary left the emergency room before she knew the outcome. A couple of years later, Mary got a phone call from the other mom who told that her son "Bubba" was alive because of that fateful day in the emergency room when God brought the two of them together. Bubba had Kendra's liver, and Mary learned that two of Kendra's other organs went to others who were dying. Mary, who is black, and Bubba's family, who are white, are all now joined at the hip, or should I say by Kendra's liver. They keep in touch regularly and attend family reunions together. There is no color barrier when it comes to love. This story was so inspiring I featured it on "Inside Out" on HTC as well as "Southern Style" on Time Warner.

Another guest I featured on "Southern Style" was Al Korman, who was fortunate to have two heart transplants. His body rejected the first after several months, and while he was being treated in the hospital for the rejection, a motorcycle accident victim's heart became available. He recounted all the wonderful things that he has since witnessed in his life since his life-saving donation, including the birth of his grandchildren. Al became active with SCOPA, as well as with the Heart Transplant Foundation, because as he attested he was truly a walking miracle.

Alma Lynne Hayden, an internationally known cross-stitch designer and former "Miss Sun Fun" who lives in Myrtle Beach, has been a guest several times to promote cross-stitching. All of her interviews have been fabulous because she is wild and crazy just like me, but her best was when she talked about becoming a kidney donor for her son. She can honestly say she gave life to him twice.

Woody Crosby was a well-known hotelier who braved the airways even though he did not want to. He was a private person, but when I explained that his interview could encourage one person to donate their organs, he agreed. Even though Woody has since passed away, he lived many extra years because someone died who cared enough to leave their organs here on earth.

Brad Dean, executive director for Myrtle Beach Area Chamber of Commerce, offered his kidney to an unknown recipient a few years ago because as Brad told me on the phone, "I only needed one, and after seeing what Woody Crosby went through, I wanted to help someone else."

Marc Jordan, Executive Director of the North Myrtle Beach Chamber, is an organ recipient who also told his story on the air with me. He said he was born once again through this experience, and that it gave him a new chance at life.

To me, this is one of the greatest opportunities I have as a journalist and broadcaster: tell the story and save lives. I continue to tell organ transplant success stories whenever I can.

THE HOLIDAY SHOW
WOLS RADIO
FLORENCE, SC

PEE DEE PEOPLE
WPDE-TV 15
FLORENCE, SC

GRAND STRAND GAZETTE
WBTW-TV 13
MYRTLE BEACH, SC

SOUTHERN STYLE
TIME WARNER CABLE
MYRTLE BEACH, SC

INSIDE OUT
HTC
CONWAY, SC

The Florence Agricultural Fair

I learned from my mentor Doug Williams to always respect the guest on the show, just like the customer service motto, "Your customers may not always be right but they are still your customers." So it goes for radio and TV, even though you can turn on any media today and see total disrespect on both sides. I believed, as Doug did, in treating all folks with respect.

There was one time, however, that I could not let something slide by that one guest said. The annual Florence Agricultural Fair was coming to town so I extended an invitation to them to come on my show. I had been going to it every single year since I moved to Florence in 1966.

The guest was the spokesperson for the fair, someone who handled the marketing of the weeklong event and traveled with the sideshow entertainment. He started out talking about the agricultural aspects of the fair, like who won the blue ribbon for the best cow, the best head of lettuce, and the best camellia. That was all well and good. He continued by talking about the new amusements like the Wild Mouse and Ferris wheel. He bragged about the corn dogs, pizza, and fried Oreo cookies. He touted the most delicious grilled corn on a stick.

Then he went into uncharted territory when he talked about the sideshows. No, I am not talking about the 400-pound Fat Lady, or the Miniature Man who looked like a munchkin from "The Wizard of Oz." He mentioned some of the risqué arenas that, according to him, were fun and innocent. He said, "There is nothing at our fair that would embarrass anyone. It is totally family-oriented."

This took me aback because I knew it was not true. Since I was a teenager, I knew, and so did everyone else, that you had to be twenty-one to get into some of the tents. Years ago, women were not even allowed in them. So I asked him, "Why do you have to be twenty-one to get in if there is nothing dirty going on?"

He said, "It's all a marketing ploy."

I was furious because I knew men who went in there and told me the illicit things that they saw. So I called him on it. He denied it and invited me to come see it. And so I agreed to go that night and report about it the next day, figuring he probably would tone down the activity knowing I was coming.

It was raunchy, very raunchy. Without going into too much detail, nude women took items from men in the audience and put them in places that should only be done in private. This was disgusting and I subtly explained that to be the case the next day on TV. I was 100% right that some parts of the fair were not family-friendly. The fair was fun and magical for local kids, but authorities should have never allowed some of the antics that went on in those tents.

The boss loved all this because he believed any controversy was good for ratings. However, it sickened me. It's another reason I never wanted to report or anchor the news. I want happy stuff: no politics, no controversy, and no more girlie shows!

PEE DEE PEOPLE
WPDE-TV 15
FLORENCE, SC

Humane Societies

If you deal with animals on television you will always have poop, pee, and plenty of un-pleasantries. Where shall I begin, because I have seen it all! Let's just cover the dogs and cats from over the years.

There was the little black kitty from the St. Frances Animal Center who fit into the palm of my hand. As I was holding her, with the camera zoomed in on her sweet little face, she gave one little meow followed by a squeak of gas that resulted in a pile of loose, soupy, bowel movement. I quickly grabbed her with my left hand and held her up so she wouldn't be sitting in it, but as I lifted her she kept spilling forth like a broken and uncontrollable ice cream dispenser. It just kept coming. As my hand, lap and shoes were feeling the drippy mess, all I could say to the little kitten was, "and do you think someone is going to want you now? I don't think so!"

It was after that that I started doing all animal interviews with a towel, or apron on my lap. After all, I still had to tape three shows after that one, so I had to go to the ladies room and rinse my pants out in warm water, roll them in a towel and put them back on! Thank goodness for me that I had worn my stretchy Chico slacks that day and not something I couldn't wash out.

Then there's the Halloween doggie fashion show I did with Diamonds In The Ruff, a business that caters to the most exquisitely attired canines. These little ones were absolutely precious: one dressed like a princess, one in a fur coat and hat, a French can-can dancer, and a bathing beauty. Each one was more gorgeous than the next. The only problem was that with their keen sense of smell, they each sniffed the carpet and could smell all the doggies that had gone before them, if you'll excuse the pun. They would prance onto the center of the set looking so beautiful, sniff, and then pee as if on cue. One walked right

255

over, lifted his leg, and pee-peed on the decorative pumpkin along the side of my chair! That's what you get with animals! However, I continued to invite them back because it makes for great television, not to mention I am an animal lover.

Then there was the dog named "Lucky" from the Humane Society of North Myrtle Beach who never stopped licking his testicles. For six minutes straight, that's all he did. Oh, I kept trying to pet his head and divert his attention to other things, but he didn't seem to care about anything else. I made a joke that they should call him Babe Ruth because of his interest in "balls!"

How about the big black Labrador that kept humping my leg during the entire segment? I would push him down trying to ignore him, but he just would not stop. That is probably how this full-blooded beauty wound up at the shelter in the first place!

One day the Grand Strand Humane Society brought in a three-legged dog. He was kind of shaggy, a mixed breed but very sweet. The lady from the shelter said they almost euthanized him because he was in bad shape when he arrived, but he was too sweet to let go.

While she and I were chatting about this dog, which I named "Tripod," our next guest, Sherry Evans, arrived and our little doggie was pulling away to get to her. He started to moan and then bark, and desperately wanted to get to her. Not viciously, just being friendly. So I asked her to come join us and as she did, he jumped in her lap and stared licking her all over. This was love at first sight. To this day, I have never seen anything like it. This guest with tears in her eyes said, "I have never owned a dog in my life because I have a house full of antiques, but I'm not leaving here without Tripod." It was puppy love for sure, and I was thrilled to be a part of it.

Thank you to all the humane societies for making sure I had a weekly segment on animals that needed to be adopted: The Grand Strand Humane Society, the Humane Society of North Myrtle Beach, The St. Frances Animal Center of Georgetown, Horry County Animal Care, Waccamaw Animal Rescue Mission, and all the other facilities who did what they could for the betterment of animal kind. A special thanks to Martha Canterbury of the Grand Strand Humane Society for being the first of local animal activists to set the stage. She was a saint!

SOUTHERN STYLE
TIME WARNER CABLE
MYRTLE BEACH, SC

Martha Canterbury

Bunny Slotchin

"Reach To Recovery" is a program sponsored by the American Cancer Society that sends women who have had breast cancer to visit and support other women who have recently been diagnosed with the disease. Bunny Slotchin from Surfside Beach appeared on TV with me many years ago long before "Reach To Recovery" with her own version called "Bosom Buddies." She described the horror a woman feels when she is facing all the unanswered questions about cancer, and the joy Bunny gets in bringing them the good news that if it is caught early, life can be beautiful again.

Bunny was very open and honest on the air about her own surgery, about her feelings and fears, and about the treatment she incurred. "Of course I worried about how I would feel after the surgery," she said. "But frankly, that right breast got in the way of my golf swing!" Then she stood up and pretended to swing a club. "Not only do I play a better game of golf now, I learned that I didn't need that breast. Besides that, my husband Ira is a leg man!"

It was Bunny's sense of humor that was so endearing. It reminds me of that old saying, "When life gives you a lemon, squeeze it and make lemonade." Bunny's lemonade was fresh and straight from the heart. She inspired me and I know she inspired every viewer. There is no doubt that she made a difference every time she walked into a hospital room to meet with a new cancer patient, or to speak to a group of women. To be able to share your personal testimony with strangers and relive the horror over and over is simply an amazing gift. The interview also covered the importance of self-breast exams and annual mammograms in order to detect cancer early.

Bunny continued her work with breast cancer patients for more than a decade. Occasionally, I would run into her around town and she was always so upbeat and optimistic. On one occasion, I was emceeing a fashion show for the Deerfield Women's Association, and who was there prancing around on the runway … Bunny! She even began a new career in her mid-60s as a watercolorist, taking lessons from Susan Duke. I recall attending an art show one Saturday at Myrtle Square Mall, and I spotted Bunny, who appeared to be working there.

"What are you doing here?" I asked her.

"It's never too late to do something you love," she said.

I was so inspired by her, as well as her paintings, that I left the art show that day with two originals by Bunny Slotchin that I simply treasure.

Bunny has since passed away but surely left footprints on the hearts of everyone who knew her. Thank you, Bunny for sharing and caring.

SOUTHERN STYLE
TIME WARNER CABLE
MYRTLE BEACH, SC

Look -Alike Contest

After I had been hosting and producing "Pee Dee People" for more than a year, I wanted to drum up some excitement so I came up with the idea of having a look-alike contest where folks would send in photos and say who it was they resembled, making them eligible for a $1,000 prize. The boss was hesitant at first, but when I offered to go out and get the sponsor, a car dealer who would front the $1,000, he realized we had nothing to lose.

The promotion was super successful. We had fifty-two entries in six weeks, some ridiculous, others simply amazing. I hung the photos all over my office and we used them on the air each week to heighten enthusiasm for the project. A top six were featured on my show and chosen by staff, but Mickey Spillane picked the winner.

Look-alikes included Julie Sierra of Fayetteville, North Carolina, as Elizabeth Taylor; Eddie Floyd of Boardman, North Carolina, as Mr. T.; Roshell Graves of Marion, South Carolina, as Janet Jackson; Misi Mather of Myrtle Beach, South Carolina, as Melissa Gilbert; Joan Cooper of Kingstree, South Carolina, as Diana Ross; and the winner was Marion Shaw, a high school coach from Aynor, South Carolina, who was a dead ringer for Craig Stadler, the golfer.

Now the funny part of this is that I knew all the celebrities except this one. When the entry arrived in the mail, I had to look up Craig Stadler and sure enough, Coach Shaw was his twin.

When I called the top six to come on the show for the finale, Coach Shaw did not know what I was talking about. He must have thought I was nuts. He figured one of his students sent it in. There is no doubt he owed that student a chunk of the $1,000.

We also had two look-alikes for Barbra Streisand and Gary Coleman, three for Kenny Rogers, a Joe Namath, a Gene

Wilder, one for Sally Field, Captain Kangaroo, Burt Reynolds, Paul Newman, and even an Edith Bunker, Jean Stapleton. This promotion was so much fun and would be a lot easier today with computer technology and e-mail entries. It brought great recognition to my show and boosted ratings when my little ol' local ABC talk show was trying to beat "Love Connection" on CBS. We did it!

PEE DEE PEOPLE
WPDE-TV 15
MYRTLE BEACH, SC

Commercials

My mentor Doug Williams told me I was a natural fit to do TV commercials. He had no idea that as a kid I use to memorize commercials and perform them for my grandfather, who thought I was terrific. I memorized the Crest commercial, the Alka Seltzer spot, and my favorite was Buster Brown. I remember using my hairbrush as a microphone and delivering the lines in front of the full-length mirror behind the bedroom door until I had every nuance perfect. I knew I would be good at this! So, from the first day Doug introduced me to WBTW's production manager, I was excited about the possibilities ahead.

In the early '70s, I was the only local woman on TV doing commercials and folks must have thought I was banking a bundle. But I made about ten commercials before I ever got paid for one. I just wanted to get my foot in the door. Once the producer got to know me, I was offered $5 for a voiceover and $10 for on-camera work. That's pitiful isn't it? But I did it anyway and loved it. WBTW TV 13 was located way out on TV Road in Florence about 12 miles from my home so it wasn't even worth the drive. It was about three years later that I requested $25 for on-camera work and got it.

My early clients were very faithful to me, especially since I was a novelty with only men doing commercials in the market. I soon became the Harvin and Gamecock meat girl, the Sumter Dairies girl, the Shrimper Restaurant girl, and Rainwater's Furniture spokesperson, which was the client I represented the longest until they closed the store due to retirement thirty years later.

As the years went on, I was able to boost my rates. Out of market rates were better, too. Soon I was doing Piggly Wiggly out of Charleston, Reese Motors in Hartsville, Boyle Toyota in Sumter, Pete Olmstead AMC-Jeep-Renault in Columbia,

Wingate Travel in Columbia, an Eye Care facility in Charlotte, Cherokee Toyota in Florence, and others. Yes, at one time in the '90s I was representing six different car dealers throughout the region at the same time.

Since I was always a good ad-libber, I was even hired to do live commercials during car-sell-athons. I went to Greensboro to do live commercials for a Toyota dealership for five hours. They flew me in and out in the same day, so I only missed one day of work at WPDE. I even did one for a grand opening of a Myrtle Beach restaurant where I was live during every commercial break for eight hours.

"Come on down here RIGHT NOW! We are waiting for you!"

Most of my clients were wonderful people, the kind of folks you would be proud to represent. But there were a few I wanted to strangle. One in particular was Cardell Carter, a car dealer in Florence. The tagline was "Cardell Carter, he's a good ol' boy."

Cardell used to do his own commercials until a marketing guru told him he was too bold and arrogant on the air and should soften it up a bit. That's when WBTW asked me to do his commercials. I agreed and would show up on the lot with the camera crew monthly and do two spots at one time. But Cardell was constantly jerking us around, changing the copy every time we arrived even though we had a script that was already approved by him. He would ask me to sit down in his office and work up a better script for him than the one the writers at the station had done. Fortunately, I was a good writer. But this was time-consuming for all of us. Soon I realized he was flirting with me and making passes that I did not appreciate and I was quickly learning that he was NOT "a good ol' boy."

One afternoon while we were there shooting a spot, I saw Cardell get mad at a man who was not accepting a car price that Cardell was offering and out of anger, Cardell grabbed the man's car keys out of his hand and threw them on the roof of the dealership. I was furious and in shock to see this client mistreated. I proudly walked over to Cardell and said I had seen the whole episode and I was no longer interested in representing him as a good ol' boy, which was far from the truth. I apologized to the camera crew, who cheered me on, and went home. It made me feel good to do that. I had heard so many horror stories about this man since doing his commercials for the past year, I felt empowered.

Hoping the station manager would understand, I called him that day and explained that I hope they would not lose the sale, even though TV 13 was the only station in the market at the time, but between the sexual innuendos and his obnoxiousness, I deserved better. Mr. Joe Foster simply said, "You have balls, DeVaughn, I'll give ya that!"

In the '80s, I landed a decent contract with Advance Advertising in Augusta, Georgia, as the spokesperson for Milton Reuben Chevrolet. "The whole town's talkin' bout Milton Reuben Chevrolet." That was the famous tagline.

I went to there once a year and did an entire year's worth of spots in one day, with a little bit of a country twang at their request and a cowgirl hat. It was always fun and well organized. However, one year there was a terrible accident on the highway outside the dealership and helicopters hovered for hours to take folks to the hospital. There was no way we could record audio with ambulance sirens in the background so I had to stay over an additional night. That gig lasted about five years and I hated to see it end. They were all wonderful folks to know and work with.

I was also the Chapin Department Store spokesperson from 1987 until they closed, thanks to Renee Lee, marketing director. I appeared in all their TV ads and hosted all their fashion shows. This was always so much fun because all the Chapin employees were one big happy family under the direction of Chapin President Harold Clardy.

For about fifteen years I was the recycling spokesperson on TV for the Horry County Solid Waste Authority: "Reduce, Reuse, Recycle." I stood in tons of trash at the landfill to do a spot once, and almost threw up. The stench was horrific. However, most of these spots were filmed at recycling centers where I would try to get customers to talk to me on camera. Men had no problem with it, but it was always hard to get a woman to do it because most of the time they would not have their makeup on or look their best while dumping trash or recyclables. People all over town recognized me as "the garbage lady" and I was quick to correct them that I was "the recycling lady."

WBTV in Charlotte hired me on several occasions for commercials, even though I hated to drive in Charlotte, but the pay was better than the local stations were paying, of course. Just like most stations, they always wanted me to be there "tomorrow," but I had two jobs I had to balance and could not always rush up to Charlotte.

One of my biggest commercial jobs that ran nationally was "Tea Time at the Master's," a cookbook produced to raise money for The Junior League and local charities featuring recipes from famous golfers. My favorite line in the sixty-second commercial was "and you'll love Arnold Palmer's zucchini bread!" This spot was shot in Augusta but ran for several years on the USA network. "Call 1-800-USA-1000 for your copy today!" I have to admit, it was thrilling to finally see myself on national TV!

A funny story about shooting that commercial was that the Junior Leaguers, after seeing my commercial demo tape, asked me to darken my hair so that I did not look like a "bleached blonde." They said they wanted me to look preppy and softer! Of course, I did as they asked, but one week later, I had it highlighted again. After all, who wants to look preppy and softer? I've always had more fun being a blonde!

Another national opportunity I had with commercials still running today is for PhysAssist Foot Pain Cream. My company Stages Video Productions produces the commercials here in Myrtle Beach and they run all over the country on cable networks, and plugged into local programs throughout the United States. This client flew me to Palm Beach, Florida, where I even appeared on a nationally syndicated cable show on the Lifetime Channel promoting the entire line of PhysAssist products. That was a thrill.

I have always been proud to represent the Horry-Georgetown Home Builders Association and their annual Home Show. For more than twenty years I have done just what they asked me to do, and that was to be silly and sell the show. In the spots I have mowed the lawn, painted walls, leaped out of bed with curlers in my hair, jumped out of the shower with a towel and shower cap on, been the face on the clock promoting "it's TIME for the Home Show," and other crazy antics. But silly does sell and I am the "queen of silly!" I am so grateful that they still want me after all these years.

CuraLase Laser Therapy hired me to do TV and radio commercials for them right after they opened their first office because I had been a client who found success and pain relief from the treatment. It was easy to sell because I believe in it, but it was hard to do something so serious after all the lighter work I had done. Yet I still help them promote their amazing laser by writing articles for them in local and regional publications.

There have been many freebies I have done during my career for nonprofit organizations. Most recently, Help 4 Kids and Back Pack Buddies asked me to get involved with them and their Vienna Sausage Campaign, and I was thrilled to do it. This organization pays no salaries, as it is made up of an all-volunteer army of folks under the direction of Barbara Mains, its guardian angel.

It takes talent to be able to be theatrical, over the top, bigger than life in a TV commercial and still appear truthful about the product you are selling. It is not as easy as it looks. We have all seen spots that are simply obnoxious, and the talent, or spokesperson, is a turn-off. Thanks to all my clients who allowed me to represent them thirty seconds at a time them over the years. Thank goodness though, I have always been a decent writer. I can't tell you how many times in the early '70s and even the '80s I wrote or re-wrote the thirty-second TV commercial on the spot with the client, because either there was no script or the client was not happy with it when we arrived to shoot. Part of the problem is that the production department knows that the salespeople want this commercial on the air as soon as possible. "Get it done and get the funds" I once heard a sales manager say to a commercial producer. Therefore, they rush writing a script with very little creativity. I found this to be a huge issue over the years. Just because someone is a good cameraman or editor does not mean they are a good writer. My husband Chuck is one of the few I know who can do it all.

It is through advertising that stations make their money. Local, regional, and national accounts pay the way. Clients can pick when they want the spots to air, or they can buy a cheaper package called ROS, or run of schedule. Usually there is a fee to make the commercial and another to run it. Many times, especially during the recent recession, stations were producing spots free just to get clients on the air and literally hovered over them so they would not pull away and move to another station. The business is viciously competitive. Fortunately for me, I still get offered opportunities to be a local television spokesperson every now and then, though certainly not as many as years ago. Who knows, one of these days I may get a call to represent a product like "Depends" and I'll be the right age for it!

Technical Difficulties

In network TV there are so many employees, cameramen, technicians, producers, grips, assistants to each of them, and even assistants to the assistants. In local TV, we are lucky enough to have a team to get you on the air. There have been way too many technical difficulties to mention, but here are a few.

In the early '70s, as I was hosting a live telethon for the March of Dimes at WBTW TV-13 in Florence and the teleprompter girl could not run the machine properly. She started out very slow, then sped it up, then went crazy, and knocked the roll right off the moving track. This was not information that I could ad-lib because it was about infant mortality in South Carolina and the high risk of birth defects. So after the prompter roll landed on the floor as I was trying to read it with some dignity, I said "Excuse me friends, the scripted info has just landed on the floor so I am going to grab it and read it to you first hand." I bent down and picked up the roll, found my place where I had left off reading and continued to unroll this bulky bit of detail in order to get the message to the viewers. Today, news anchors control their own prompters, without the roll of paper as well.

While hosting "Pee Dee People" for WPDE TV 15 in 1981, one of our cameras died while we were live. The cameraman kept trying to tell me something but I did not know what he was trying to say while I tried to pay attention to the interview I was conducting with the local cancer society. So I simply asked the guest to excuse me for a moment, asked the cameraman to shout out what he wanted me to know and then I asked the guest to move closer to me so that they could cover us with both with the two working cameras. No need to be so formal, or nervous about it, just do what you have to do, and move on!

In the mid-'80s while doing "Southern Style," I worked for ten years with no tally lights on the camera. Those are the lights that tell the on-air person which camera was on the air at the time. I never knew which camera was up unless I looked at the monitor in the studio, a small TV where I was actually watching what was on the air live.

Another weird episode when I first started hosting "Southern Style" was that we sometimes would pick up the WKZQ radio frequency which distorted our audio while we tried to broadcast live. None of our so-called engineers could figure it out. That lasted for longer than a year. Additionally, the tin roof on the building made a horrendous noise when it rained. Cable subscribers would call the station and report some sort of interference during their viewing of the show. We hated to tell them that it was simply rain hitting the roof. After all, the building was originally for storing cable, not for doing TV.

During a live interview with an alcohol and drug abuse counselor during "Southern Style" in 1985, all the lights in the studio went out following a big boom-like noise. Just when I thought we were knocked off the air, the director yelled, "Keep talking! We are still on the air!" So I told the viewers we would continue with the interview even though we didn't have any lights and I hoped they would just pretend we were on the radio! We finished the last ten minutes in total darkness.

While doing a stir-fry cooking segment on "Southern Style" in 1986, the studio started to fill up with smoke, which caused the smoke alarms to go off. It was so loud I could barely hear the guest. But the crew and I knew that the place was not on fire, so we did not exit the building but kept the cameras rolling instead. We explained to the viewers that the fire department would be arriving any minute to turn off the obnoxious noise. So we just kept talking and cooking. Finally, the firemen arrived and turned off the alarm. As they stuck their heads into the studio, I apologized and invited them to come over and taste the food we had just made. I ended the show with three handsome firemen in their heavy gear munching on stir-fry.

More technical difficulties happen with microphones than anything else, which is why sometimes on the major networks you will see anchors with two microphones clipped to their clothing. I have had production folks sneak in during the middle of an interview and hand me a new mic to clip onto a guest, or onto myself if mine went out.

One thing is very clear about the production staff – they can make you look great or they can make you look bad. I kissed up to them whenever possible. Often though, in low-budget local TV, the lighting is poor, the sound is less than adequate, and the equipment can be antiquated. In my career, I have experienced it all, but here is one that takes the cake.

So what do you do when thirty minutes before you are going live and the police arrive and give you the name of your director who they need to see right away? At first you panic. Secondly, you go over and calm down the guests who are arriving, and assure the rest of the crew that you are sure everything will be okay. Yes, I have always been a positive thinker. Yet, in this case, the police walked out of master control with our director by the arm and said they were taking him to jail for not paying child support. "But officers, could you let him stay through the show which is live at 10 a.m.?" They laughed, and so did our director. Well, you can't blame a girl for trying! But on the way out both of the officers told me how much they loved the show and watched it every night, as it was repeated at 7:30 p.m. They said they would surely be tuned in tonight to see what happens now that they were taking our director off to jail! "We're sorry, Diane. Just doing our job!"

Immediately I called our production manager, Nat Adams, who was still at home at that time but he thought I was joking. We were a big joking crowd at Cox Cable during the mid- to late '80s, so I didn't blame him. As I begged him to come fast, he was still laughing, saying that he wasn't going to fall for this! I had to get one of the guests to come to the phone to verify what had just happened.

Luckily, Nat lived in Pine Lakes and made it to the studio five minutes before airtime. We went on as scheduled with our guest who was discussing alcohol addictions and we opened the phone lines as planned. Wouldn't you know it, we had a woman call in pretending to be drunk. After she refused to hang up so we could go on to other callers, I finally hung up on her myself.

It was always sad that a few people took folly in screwing with our live call-in shows. Between our director going to jail and the drunken lady on the phone, I was wiped out when the show was finally in the can!

On my very first taping for my current show "Inside Out," I had a big technical difficulty. As the crew and I were backing out of a strawberry field where we were filming Sid Thompson of Thompson Farms, we backed into a ditch. Sid had to get his big tractor to haul us out. So, I decided to have the crew video Sid hauling us out of the ditch. Then I ended the interview by saying "This is what happens when city-folk come to the country!" Let's face it, in this business you have to be able to laugh at yourself and know that technical difficulties are part of it all.

MARCH OF DIMES TELETHON
WBTW-TV 13
FLORENCE, SC

PEE DEE PEOPLE
WPDE-TV 15
FLORENCE, SC

SOUTHERN STYLE
COX CABLE/TIME WARNER CABLE
MYRTLE BEACH, SC

HTC
INSIDE OUT
CONWAY, SC

A Salute to Chuck

Sometimes I feel like the luckiest woman on earth to have such a sweet, adorable, supportive husband. Actually I am. Chuck and I are together more hours of the day than most couples as we work together and play together. Our partnership at Stages Video Productions been simply flawless, and with him directing my TV show "Inside Out" on HTC, we are magically connected everyday. But that's not all we have in common:

We both love to travel and have visited many glorious destinations in the world. We are both very family oriented and our faith guides us everyday. One other passion we share is theater, not just attending shows, but being in various productions together, feeding off each other's energy.

Back in 1978 I was Linda Low in the production of "Flower Drum Song" at the Florence Little Theater. It was fun, but not nearly as special as when I finally met Chuck and we were able to appear on stage together in Myrtle Beach. Chuck had been active at the Sumter Little Theater appearing in "South Pacific" and starring in "Robin Hood," and he agrees that the real thrill of performing is doing it as a team. We have done about thirty shows and musical reviews for the Theatre of the Republic in Conway, First Presbyterian Church Players, Grand Strand Senior Center and Atlantic Stage. The highlight however was "I Do! I Do!" at the Theater of the Republic, which featured just the two of us for the entire two-hour production portraying characters from the wedding day to moving to a retirement center. We literally grew old on stage, adding wrinkles, changing wigs and costumes on stage. It was directed by Lou Layton, with Liz Layton as Music Director, and backstage support by the students at the Academy of Arts, Science, and Technologies Center in Myrtle Beach. We took the show to the South Carolina Theater Competition winning the state title, and then onto to the regional competition in Florida where we competed against professional theater companies and returned home with several prestigious awards.

On our way to the state competition we almost wrecked our car as a truck filled with sludgy manure dumped it's contents on I-20 as we followed close behind. It was the smelliest mess as we slipped and slid amidst the muck. Chuck maintained control of the car, even though others went flying into a ravine. We called the highway patrol to report it but had no time to stop and get the car cleaned, as we did not want to miss our scheduled performance for the judges. However, when we pulled up at the hotel everyone, even the car park attendant, backed away from the car. We figured that the manure christening was an omen that we might as well turn around and go home. However, having won the championship, we now know it brought us luck!

Some of our funniest memories as a couple have come from theater experiences. In "I Do! I Do!" I had to wear a big stuffed apron pretending I was pregnant. One night during the play my bodysuit that was snapped at my crotch, came unsnapped and sent the apron upward. It was difficult trying to do the scene with the baby elevating with each step. Chuck could not figure out why I was lying on the bed when he knew on all other nights, I was standing next to him doing dialogue.

Another night during this show, I had to use the bathroom during intermission and forgot I was wearing a bodysuit and pee-ed right thru it. Thank goodness for hairdryers.

This show was incredibly rewarding to perform as a real-life husband and wife. We cried every night along with the audience as we grew old. It was a very heart-warming production.

Another great experience was "Hello Dolly" with the FPC Players directed by Brown Bradley as I played Dolly and Chuck was Horace. At the very end of the show one night during the run, I had forty-five seconds from one scene to the next to get into my wedding dress so three volunteers awaited me backstage to assist with the skirt, top and headdress. Well, someone forgot to attach all the Velcro strips, and so as I ran out on stage and twirled around in the final scene, the bottom portion of my wedding dress gingerly fell to the ground. My black bodysuit stood out like a sore thumb, but luckily I was wearing it!!! There was an instant standing ovation even though there was still one stanza left to sing before the show ended. Chuck just bent down and hauled it back up and held it in place as I sang "Wow, wow wow fellas, look at the old girl now, fellas!!!"

Chuck was so perfect as Charlie Brown in " You're A Good Man Charlie Brown". It was fun being the bratty and pompous "Lucy" telling Charlie Brown night after night how stupid he was and that he needed a psychiatrist. We did this show with the FPC Players. Brown Bradley directed it and starred as "Snoopy". Audiences loved seeing Brown an accomplished opera singer and former Broadway performer, crawl around the floor on all fours and sing "Suppertime". Each night Brown would try to crack me up lifting his leg as if he was going to pee on it.

Directed by Tim McGhee at The Theatre of The Republic, Chuck was sensational in "Barnum" as "P.T Barnum". He sang, danced, walked on a tightrope, swung on ropes and even walked on stilts.

I was "Mrs. Barnum" but the starring role surely belonged to Chuck. One night one of his stilts fell loose and he gracefully leaped for the front curtain and lowered himself to the floor. Chuck never skipped a beat and the audience thought it was part of the show.

He was every bit the showman as the real "P.T. Barnum".

Another memorable show for us was "Damn Yankees" with the Theatre of The Republic directed by Larry Stock. Chuck was the devil and I was Lola. What great fun to have my real-life husband encouraging me to sleep with young ball players and bring them down.

"Guys And Dolls" was the only show we did twice, but ten years apart at The Theatre of The Republic: The first time it was directed by Doris Hudson and the second time by Tim McGhee.

As Nathan and Adelaide we had a ball night after night trying to out do these over-the top personas, both endearing characters to theater lovers.

Well the list goes on. The point is we fuel each other on stage and off. We are blessed with a beautiful, loving relationship that started with a friendship at WPDE-TV 15 and stood the test of time, thirty-one years. Chuck has never resented me being in the limelight; as a matter of fact he supports it 100%. He is always by my side escorting me to all the events I have volunteered to emcee, and he is always there to cheer me on no matter what I do.

When I was named "Volunteer of the Year" for the Myrtle Beach Chamber of Commerce, I told the crowd that I shared the honor with Chuck because while I was out volunteering for them, he was back at the office covering my job and his!

So even though I may have kissed a few frogs in my past life, God finally sent my prince.

He was worth the wait.

Thank you, Chuck for all your love and support.

You're simply the best!

"Hello Dolly"

Photo:
Craig McNab

"Guys and Dolls"
Photo: Tim McGhee

"You're a Good Man Charlie Brown"

"Damn Yankees"

"I Do! I Do!"

"Barnum"

277

Closing

There were many happy remembrances as I wrote this book and recalled the wild and crazy situations that happened as the cameras rolled, but I also had many tearful moments because so many of these wonderful friends have passed away. However, you know what they say: as long as there is someone out there who remembers you, you will always live on. Most of all, this journey through the past forty-two years of my career has been heart-warming and rewarding.

A gigantic thanks to all of you who were brave enough to come before my microphones and cameras. Thanks for the memories and especially for enlightening my audiences with your time and talents. There have so many of you over the years that I could write five more books filled with other great heart warming stories. Please don't be insulted if I left any of you out. You have all been precious to me.

Finally, thank goodness this isn't good-bye because thanks to "Inside Out" that I host and produce on HTC channel 4 , and "Diane At Six" on EASY Radio, I'm still "Floating On Air!"

Matt Sedota
Blue Crab Festival

Me as Jingles the Elf
with Captain Smiley

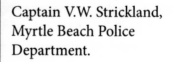

Captain V.W. Strickland,
Myrtle Beach Police
Department.

Photo:
Jack Thompson

Back:
Marv Clark, Me,
Mixon Dixon.

Front:
Sherena Gainey Deigan,
The Deacon

Myrtle Square Mall

Me, Doug Williams, Jim Griffin, Strom and Nancy Thurmond
WBTW Muscular Dystrophy Telethon

281

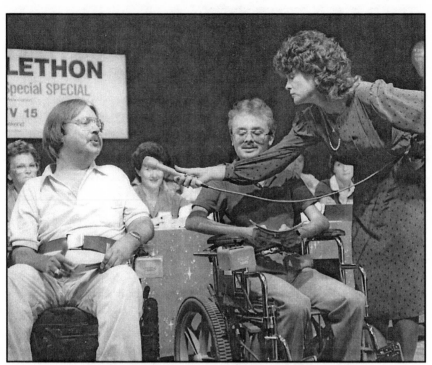

WPDE Muscular Dystrophy Telethon 1982
Photo: Donna Lawrence

WBTW Muscular Dystrophy Telethon 1977

Dixie Dugan,
Bill Daniels and me

Florence Christmas Parade 1983
Me, Rick Henry, Jan Pate, Chuck driving,
Joan Smith, Al Klench
Photo: Hartley Ferguson

Cox Cable's on-air
personalities
Glen Deigan, me,
Richard Green
1986

CPSIA information can be obtained at www.ICGtesting.com
Printed in the USA
LVOW08s1245141015

458196LV00004B/4/P